MILLENNIAL
WORKFORCE

Cracking the Code to
Generation Y in Your Company

JAVIER MONTES

ISBN: 978-1-4834-6114-4 (sc)
ISBN: 978-1-4834-6113-7 (e)

Library of Congress Control Number: 2016918669

Lulu Publishing Services rev. date: 1/24/2017

CONTENTS

DEDICATION

This book is dedicated to my 2 beautiful daughters, Melany & Tiffany, and to my gorgeous wife, Legne.

While the content in this book isn't really what I am dedicating to you, I am dedicating to you the completion of this book project. Since I have never written a book before, this was a huge undertaking for me and very intimidating. While writing this book, there were countless moments that I wanted to quit on finishing this book. Every time I contemplated giving up, the only thing that I could think of was "What would my girls think of me if they knew that I gave up? Is this the example that I want to set for my family to follow? Do I want my girls to give up on their dreams whenever things get tough?" The answer was always a resounding "No!" It was those exact moments that all three of you unknowingly gave me the strength, courage, and perseverance to keep pushing forward and not give up. I once read that "Your children will do as you do, not as you say." I think about this almost every day. It serves as a constant reminder for me to live my life in the way that I would like for you to live yours; especially during the days when I am no longer around.

I want this book to serve as a constant reminder for you to never give up on your dreams and goals. Don't let anybody, especially yourself, tell you that you can't do something. Daddy is telling you right now: You can accomplish ANYTHING that you want in life! You each have no limits. Don't be afraid or embarrassed to dream big. It takes the same amount of energy to dream big as it does to dream small. Although life will always challenge you with situations that force you out of your comfort zone, it is these exact situations that will help you grow and develop new skills and additional knowledge.

While you are still too young to ever know how much you inspire me and motivate me, I don't ever want to miss the opportunity to tell you. I pray that this message stays alive and vibrant throughout your entire lives and that it can re-appear throughout your life at the moments when you need it the most. I want you both to know that "Papi" loves you more than I will ever be able to explain, and I am very excited to spend my entire life trying to show you.

Yo si puedo!

Loving you with all my heart,

Javier Montes ("Papi")

ACKNOWLEDGEMENTS

"While Javier Montes keys on the Millennials in the workplace, the action ideas and concepts he identifies are applicable to all folks in an organization. No theory here, just good old plain experience! The Chapter on recruiting and hiring alone is worth at least 100 times the price of the book."

- Jack Daly, Amazon Best Selling Author and Selling Authority

"The Millennials are the latest generation to hit the work force, and the most misunderstood by leadership groups within most organizations. They will be the majority of the work force in the next 5 years, and in this book, Javier gives us some insight into their backgrounds, thoughts, and ideas. The book also gives leaders some specific things they can do to increase retention and engagement of their Millennials."

- John Bly, CPA, CVA, CM&AA, CGMA, CEO of LBA Haynes Strand, PLLC and Author of "Cracking the Code: An Entrepreneur's Guide to Growing your Business Through Mergers and Acquisitions for Pennies on the Dollar"

"Wow! So many practical insights into the Millennial mindset. There is huge take-away value from this book."

- Noah B. Rosenfarb, CPA/ABV/PFS

"Millennials are the future of businesses both as employees and customers. Montes shows the keys to unlocking their potential, what buttons to push and avoid for your business to capitalize on this powerful group."

- John R. DiJulius III author of The Customer Service Revolution

"Millennials are smart, hard working and they are the driving force of the future. They can also be a pain in the neck if you don't understand them. If you want to succeed you need to learn how to communicate and lead millennials. Javier lays it out nicely so we can all understand how his experience working with millennials has grown his business. Read this book if you want to grow your business."

- Joe Apfelbaum CEO, Ajax Union

"Javier Montes conveys the strengths and benefits of millennials with insight and passion. He offers detailed methods to create a workplace that enhances their abilities and keeps them engaged and contributing. Finally, his comprehensive hiring strategy insures you hire the millennial who is an exact fit for your company and will remain a loyal team member. His personal experience makes him an expert to follow."

- Sandy Fox, Owner, Investment Copy

PREFACE

While all of my friends were partying and enjoying their college experience, I was busy taking eighteen credits per semester in university, working full-time, and building my business. Those were not easy years, but I can still say that I enjoyed every second.

Through the bad times and difficult situations, I got to where I am now. I largely attribute this success to my unwavering persistence. Today, I am the proud owner of a growing business, and the leader of an amazing team that consists entirely of millennials.

Many believe that millennials are lazy, entitled, unmotivated and tend to jump from one opportunity to another. However, I have found them to be hard working, dedicated, innovative, and profitable. Indeed, they are the secret to my success! And there's an unexpected benefit. When I invested time and effort into training and developing them, not only did their skills improve, but also – quite unanticipated – I learned something from every millennial at the same time. Our collaboration and relationship are mutually beneficial in more ways than one. Not for one second would I entertain the idea of exchanging them for non-millennials.

In this book, I will share everything that I have done in my business that helped me build an amazing, motivated, hardworking, and dedicated team. I will go further. I will also share the reasoning and arguments behind each of these decisions. This is done with the hopes that you can immediately implement the methodologies that you want in your own team, as well as understand why you want to use them and why they will work. Because you understand the reasoning, you will be able to customize or personalize my techniques to your individual company in the way that you feel will work best.

Should you be left with any additional questions after finishing the book, please reach out to me via my website: www.MeetJavierMontes. com. There, you will also find a number of resources, which will guide you in your journey to creating a dedicated and motivated team of your own millennials. You will be equipped to tap into this unmined resource of talent to the envy of your competitors.

CHAPTER 1

UNDERSTANDING MILLENNIALS

BEFORE WE BEGIN to break down the mental DNA of a millennial, it's only fitting that we define who a millennial is. By definition, the millennial generation was born between 1980 and 2000. "Millennial" was the term coined simply because they were being born just before the turn of the millennium. This group is also less commonly known as "Generation Y"—a continuation of the preceding "Generation X."

For the past decade, Gen Xers and baby boomers have been hot topics of discussion in the business world, due to the enormous size of their populations. Ironically, most of us don't realize that millennials (Generation Y) is currently the largest population in the United States. In 2016, they surpassed the baby boomers, and the trend has only grown. Dan Christian Roehm & Noah Rosenfarb wrote an amazing book about planning for succession in your business titled 20/20 Vision: Who Will Own Your Company in 2020? While the book provides four possible answers, sourced from their clients' various first-hand experiences, it left one final option of "OTHER." I am going to propose that, within a few short years, the correct answer might be millennials.

It's important to note that by the year 2020, millennials will account for more than 50 percent of the entire U.S. workforce. Like it or not, it is highly probable that half of your company will be made up of this younger generation. This statistics says at least 50 percent of the people applying for jobs at your company are going to be millennials. By 2030, millennials will represent a full 75 percent of the global workforce. In order to stay successful, all managers, entrepreneurs, and organization leaders will have to learn how to understand, embrace, and effectively leverage this generation.

"By 2020 Millennials will make up 50% of the U.S. workforce and will increase to 75% by 2030."

Most of the business leaders I speak with today have little-to-no experience working with this generation and they remain nervous about bringing a millennial into their companies. Because of all the negative things they have heard, some business managers even go to great lengths to avoid hiring a millennial. I have found this to be a case of fearing the unknown. This extreme is not necessary— a millennial is simply a member of another (often misunderstood) generation. If we can analyze the way that this generation thinks and acts, we can capitalize on them and use their unique strengths to boost our companies... just as I've done in my business.

JUMPING INTO THE MIND OF A MILLENNIAL

My intention in writing this book is to share my extensive experience with millennials in my own business. I wanted to explain how I have seen overwhelming success by working almost exclusively with this generation.

Over the last few years, a number of entrepreneurs and industry leaders have informally interviewed me about my young team. I've often been asked for advice about how to solve some of the common problems others face with younger employees in their companies. Initially, I felt like I wasn't doing anything special. But as these conversations increased in frequency, it became clear to me that I was, in fact, running my business in a unique way. The things that I explain throughout this book were so natural and innate to me, I never felt as though I worked to purposely create an atmosphere conducive to millennials. Yet, it did.

So, how was this possible? Where did I learn to run my business this way?

During the first few minutes of research for this book, it struck me. By definition, I am considered a millennial. I was floored! How could it be that I was considered a millennial? I didn't think or act like a millennial. I didn't reason or make decisions like a millennial. And I certainly didn't think that I related to millennials....Or did I?

I pondered this for the next few weeks, and came to realize that in effect, I was a blend of Generation X and Generation Y. I was born at the dividing line that separates the Gen Xers and the millennials, so I grew up during the same years as the millennials.

But my life experiences and the manner in which my parents raised me were much more Gen X. These shaped me in a way that caused me to think and act differently than other kids my age. And perhaps my character was different as well. For most of my life, I have been considered the oddball in my classrooms. I had many acquaintances and got along well with almost everyone, but had few close friendships. I didn't seem to have much in common with most of the other kids. One of those differences that emerged at a very young age was my entrepreneurial mind.

In my elementary school days, I loved the Christmas season. Most kids delighted in the presents under the tree; I was most excited about the day after Christmas. This was my favorite day of the year! I would ask my father and uncle to take me to the nicest neighborhoods in town so I could look through the garbage piles. Why? I knew that if a child got a new bicycle for Christmas, he would likely throw away his old bicycle, even though it may be in great working condition. I would pick up the bicycle, take it home, and clean it up a little bit. The next week, I had a good bicycle to sell at a garage sale in front of my house. This time of year only came around once, so I needed something else to do for the remaining eleven months. Here I received my first lesson in seasonality. I learned that I didn't want to have a business whose revenues would be drastically (and uncontrollably) affected by something as basic as the calendar.

Around this time, I noticed recycling growing in our city. The county installed aluminum can recycling machines where you inserted cans into the machine and the machine gave you money! The more cans that you brought, the more money you got. I started saving all the aluminum cans that my family used during parties and gatherings. I stored them in big garbage bags, then recycled them and enjoyed my cash. But the process was way too slow. I needed to find a faster way to collect more cans.

My parents had a nice condo on Miami Beach and my family spent many weekends on the beautiful sand. Do you know how many people take canned sodas and beers to the beach? While other kids were having fun splashing around and building sand castles, I enjoyed walking up and down the beach collecting cans from every trash can I passed. Yes, I was the "weird kid." I would walk miles down the beach and not come back until I'd filled at least two trash bags. I recruited my brother and cousins to come work with me. I gave them each two trash bags, and we would cover more ground in less time. One team would go north, and the other would go south.

It was here that I learned a powerful lesson about creating competition to motivate your team. The contest was: which team would fill up the trash bags faster? Everyone felt encouraged and had a lot of fun each day. At the end of the weekend, I loaded up my parents' truck with eight to ten garbage bags full of cans, return home, and collect my big payout.

"…I learned a powerful lesson about creating competition to motivate your team."

When I was just twelve years old, I wanted to capitalize on my passion for music and become a DJ. I asked my father to lend me $3,000 to purchase my first equipment. He thought I was crazy and refused to hand over so much money. After about six months of bothering him, he finally gave in loaned me the money. The caveat was that I had to pay back every last penny. I was excited about the opportunity and immediately got to work marketing myself. Exactly one year later, I paid my father the last hundred dollars of his original investment. This simple life experience taught me many lessons in the business world. I learned about sales, marketing, referrals, and the power of leverage. Most important, I learned what it was to be an entrepreneur.

During high school, I attended an athletic school. All of the school's sports programs were reigning champions. Most of the students were big on exercising and nutrition and many of them got hungry before it was time for lunch. If the students failed to bring a snack from home, there was nowhere to get food. I saw an opportunity. Once a week, McDonald's offered Egg McMuffin sandwiches for thirty-nine cents. On Wednesdays, I would wake up early, call the local McDonald's, and place an order for fifty Egg McMuffins. The local McDonald's prepared my order before I arrived. I picked up the sandwiches and took them to school in a gym bag. Word spread quickly among the hungry students that I had hot breakfast sandwiches for sale for a dollar. I usually sold all fifty sandwiches within the first hour. Although I was making a very good return on my investment, I could only do this the one day a week that McDonald's offered the discount.

Then, McDonald's stopped offering the special and my entire business plan went down the drain! This was not going to stop me—my customers needed my products and services. I polled my customers to find out what type of sandwich they enjoyed the most. The vast majority said they loved a good ham and cheese sandwich. I quickly went to work and made ten sandwiches for my first day of work, to see whether my customers would like the product. I sold out within ten minutes. Within a few days, I had sourced the best prices for ham, cheese, bread, mayo, and mustard. Every day, I woke up two hours early and prepared seventy sandwiches to sell to my customers. I sold to students around my class schedule and typically sold out by 11 am.

The school faculty objected to me selling sandwiches during school time. They began to confiscate my gym bags and punish me with detention. I was giving myself away as I carried four overfilled gym bags to school each day. So the faculty could easily spot me. That stopped me temporarily.

"I learned to scale and use the power of leveraging a sales team."

I realized I needed a sales team. I recruited a few of my friends, and distributed gym bags to each one in the mornings. Each of these students bought twenty sandwiches from me at a discounted rate (wholesale) and then turned around and sold the sandwiches (retail) to make a small profit. I didn't do any of the marketing work and now I was taking home more profits because I was able to move more product. This business went on for three out of my four years of high school. The only reason it stopped was because I graduated. I learned many business principles during these years. I learned:

- I should not have a business that depended on another business's promotions, because this was not scalable.
- The power of leveraging a sales team
- The government will always be an impeding factor in my growth.

Through all these years, I continued working on my DJ business on the weekends. I followed my parents' instructions as best I could: go to school, get good grades, earn a scholarship to a good university, graduate with a degree, get a job at a large company, and work my way up the corporate ladder, until one day I'd retire as the president of the company. I followed most of the steps and graduated from Florida International University with a degree in finance. I got a job at a national bank and quickly began working my way up the corporate ladder. I started as a part-time teller and within a few years was promoted to a senior bank representative.

One day, the bank did something that really upset me. I sat stewing at my desk for about twenty minutes, then decided that I would not tolerate this! I drafted up my resignation letter and immediately took it to my supervisor. She was shocked! She tried to convince me that I had a very promising career in the banking industry but I was dead set on my decision. She accepted my resignation, and that was the end of corporate America for me. I decided I would work on growing my DJ business full-time. I quit my $70,000-a-year job to finally follow my dream of working for myself.

During my first twelve months, I made total sales of just under $7,000. This might be enough to drive most people to quit, but I kept pushing forward. During the next twelve months, I doubled sales to $14,000. Over the next few years, my business grew to produce over half a million dollars in sales annually. Today, Entertainment Management Group (EMG) is one of the South Florida's most respected names in the luxury entertainment industry.

Looking back at these experiences, it is extremely hard for me to comprehend that I am a millennial. I have a much deeper connection with Gen Xers and baby boomers. All of my friends and the people with whom I clicked with were much older than me. Among the very few close friendships I have had, I can comfortably say that they were all Gen Xers. I attribute this to the way I was raised by my parents. Both of them immigrated to the United States and raised me in a household with a very traditional set of values—things that are considered today to be an old-school way of thinking. Some of these values are said to have been lost in the millennial generation.

On the other hand, I lived during the same years as millennials and experienced many of the things they lived through.

I found myself to be an extremely unique breed and decided to blend the two: I now call myself an "X-Millennial! I can serve as a bridge to firmly connect the two generations, because I have the gift of understanding and communicating with both generations in a way that few others can. I think and make decisions like a Gen Xer because of the way I was raised. At the same time, I grew up in the digitally advanced, technological age as a millennial, so I can share the same life experiences. Although I had never really appreciated being "the odd one out" while growing up, it is now my biggest asset. Using this, I am able to connect these two different generations that have been struggling to effectively communicate.

GROWING UP AS A MILLENNIAL

In order for you to comprehend why millennials think and act the way they do, you need to understand what growing up was like for these children. What world did they experience growing up?

Participation Was Enough

This generation's kids were put into sports teams and extracurricular activities by their parents, so they could develop new skills and abilities. Sounds the same as previous generations, right? It is, except for one very different variable.

"If you want to be the winner, you need to out-work the loser."

During these years, a huge shift occurred, where everyone suddenly worked to protect a child's self-esteem. The media told young parents, "A child with low self-esteem is more likely to have suicidal thoughts later on in life." Of course, this is enough to terrify any parent. A domino effect followed, until coaches and teachers felt pressured to avoid any actions that could possibly lower a child's self-esteem. At the end of baseball season, everyone on the team suddenly had to receive an award. No longer were coaches able to truly recognize the above-average performers. They were forced to come up with a creative way to acknowledge every single child on the team for something, simply to ensure that they all received an equal award. This may have made sense to the parents, but they were robbing their children of a very valuable life lesson: there are always winners and losers. If you want to be the winner, you need to out-work the loser.

Millennials were unfortunately taught that all you have to do is show up and participate, and you will be rewarded. In previous generations, there had always existed clear winners and losers— you would get a reward only when you excelled. But this generation never had that experience.

Music

When millennials started evolving into their adolescent years, portable MP3 music players (e.g., iPods) were just being introduced to the world. Music became easily accessible, and cemented its presence in this generation's daily life.

The entire wave began when the Internet gained traction, and people could download music from Napster. I'm sure you remember that name. Because of this, most millennials will connect to music on a much deeper level than generations before. This is why you will typically see young adults with headphones in their ears throughout most of the day; it's how they feel most at peace and focused. It's become an integral part of their way of life. Unfortunately, video (versus audio) didn't become such a central figure in their lives, but this is only because during those years it was not as easily "streamable" as it is today. It's important to note that incorporating music into your office culture can make millennials feel more at home.

Instant Gratification

Thinking back to Napster and the ability to download files, we realize that after the turn of the century, instant gratification became a big part of our lives. We no longer needed to send something off in the mail and waiting for it to come back. If you wanted to buy an item, you went online. You could either download it immediately or place an order, and it soon showed up at your doorstep. Young adults today have the gift of Amazon, where one-click ordering can have a product delivered in as quickly as two hours.

This is an important characteristic of the millennial generation. These adults grew up when the world provided them what they needed, or even simply wanted, almost instantly. They lived in a society that taught them to expect instant gratification in all aspects of their lives. For Gen X, this started to happen when microwaves gained popularity.

"Millennials were born into a world where they never had to wait…not even for water to boil!"

Imagine that you've never had to wait for water to boil. Imagine only knowing how to heat water in a few seconds with a microwave. This is the world into which the millennials were born. In this generation, they've always gotten access to things very quickly, and they didn't experience some of the struggles that the previous generations encountered.

For example, let's talk about cassette tapes for recording audio. Kids from Gen X would prepare a blank cassette tape inside the radio recorder and wait until the radio played the song of their choice. Then they'd rush to the radio, hit record, and hope they got the beginning of the song so that they could replay it whenever they wanted. Millennials have no idea what this concept is all about. Why? Because if they wanted music, they went online and downloaded it, and had it available right away. The same was true with videotapes. If you wanted to re-watch a movie once it finished, Gen X had to rewind and wait. Millennials don't know what that is. They simply pressed the menu button on their DVD remote, and it played again. If they wanted to skip forward or back, or watch a certain scene, it was a mere button push away. Millennials grew up with things like DVRs, where they could watch things whenever they want to watch them. This generation didn't have much experience with TV Guide and having to plan and schedule viewing time during the week. This generation says, "No, I want to watch it now. I turn on my DVR, or I turn on my Netflix, and I get to watch it right now."

Another example is the telephone. When millennials were in their adolescent years, cell phones were a normal thing. A physical landline, connected to the wall, served no purpose to them. For decades, if you wanted to communicate with someone, you had to wait until they got home or to work. Millennials have never experienced that. They want to talk to somebody now, so they pick up their cell phone, call that somebody's cell phone, and they answer immediately. Millennials live on text messaging because "I expect a response now." That has always been their standard. They don't really understand the concept of having to wait for things, because never in their lives have they been forced to wait for anything.

The things that Gen Xers would consider advanced technology are the same things that millennials consider to be standard. Through no fault of their own, millennials have lived with instant gratification for every aspect of their lives.

Helicopter Parents

Most millennials grew up with helicopter parents. Foster Cline and Jim Fay coined this phrase in the early 2000s and it gained popularity as the millennial generation reached college age. It described parents who would hover over their children—like a helicopter—protecting and constantly watching them. For example, if the child got bad grades in school, the parent would blame the teacher and essentially "save the child". If the child were in a sporting event, the parent would hover over to make sure the child was treated fairly and didn't get skipped over. These children became dependent on their parents to swoop in and save the day... to be their protectors and bodyguards. This created a very strong bond between child and parent, though it made the relationship more like friends than a typical, authoritative hierarchy.

When millennials created this bond with their parents, it obscured the line of respect going upward or downward.

Millennials question things, call out their peers, and challenge authority. This generation does not intend to be disrespectful or rude. It's simply that they grew up in an age where they can quickly and definitively answer any question on Google. They are unaccustomed to anything being an unknown. They are used to relying on search engines.

> **"Millennials question things, call out their peers, and challenge authority…they're just trying to learn and fully understand concepts."**

If an authority figure tells them something, they do not immediately accept it as truth. They would probably google it themselves first. Since they can go on Google and find the answer 24/7, this created the propensity for millennials to challenge authority and reject the status quo. "I don't automatically accept statements from anyone else, no matter their position. I'll check it out for myself."

That is very important to point out regarding millennials. It would be easy for us to dismiss very talented people (who would bring value to our organizations) as being unmanageable or disrespectful of authority. We need to understand that in their minds, they're just trying to learn and fully understand concepts. In today's technologically-advanced world, we must question the ways things are being done, as well as constantly challenge the status quo. Otherwise, our companies will not be able to satisfy the ever-changing needs of our innovatively demanding clients.

Millennials are naturally wired this way, and they're poking holes in things that they want to understand more clearly. They don't see any problem with that. It's not that they're obstinate or unmanageable; it's simply how they learn. As leaders, we ought to be open to this approach and leverage the millennial asset for the future vitality of our organizations.

Optimistic

One of the most valuable traits of this generation is that they are instinctively optimistic. Millennials entered adulthood during recession times, right after the real estate bubble burst in the United States. During these years, the entire world was focused on trying to rebuild the economy, and the media was talking about bright plans for the future. This generation was too young to care about the economy at the time, but they were coming of age during the rebuilding years. Because of this, they grew up very optimistic about the future. They have always looked forward positively, convinced that things would continually improve. They were convinced they could achieve things that had never been achieved before.

> **"This optimism is fantastic and, as leaders, we should tap into it to fuel our organizations."**

I'm sure you can agree that it's refreshing to have somebody like this on your team: "Yes, we can accomplish that, even though we've never done it before." "Yes, things will get better next year, next month." "Even though I've seen a trend of bad things come in the past, I know we're going to do better." This generation was exposed to a time when everywhere they turned, all they heard was, "Let's fix the economy. Let's get better!" They heard this all over the radio and the news, and things *were* getting better. Then they watched the stock market pick up, and this "nowhere to go but up" mentality became part of their psyche. Millennials exclaimed, "Hey, we're going to get through this. We got through 9/11, and we got through the financial crisis. It seems like no matter how doom and gloom it is, we always survive."

I think that led to a survival mentality where they believed they could always find a way out. This optimism is fantastic and, as leaders, we should tap into it to fuel our organizations.

Experiences Versus Possessions

This leads us into our next millennial characteristic. Because they lived during years where so many people lost their homes to foreclosures, their cars to repossessions, and their retirement savings to the stock market, millennials grew up thinking that these material possessions should be of little value. After all, they could be taken away quickly for reasons outside of their own control. For this reason, they put a much higher value on experiences, because experiences were things that could never be taken away. Gen X was very much about collecting things and believing that success was equal to the amount of possessions that one could acquire. Millennials do not think that way. A millennial values experiences a hundred times more than any possessions. They value, "What is the next best thing?"

This is the generation that came up with the hashtags #YOLO (You Only Live Once) and #FOMO (Fear of Missing Out). They don't want to miss out on anything. With social media, they are watching what their friends are doing all across the world. They want to boast about where they ate last night and where they are going next week. Their life values are centered around experiences and not possessions. This is important for us to know about millennials. As we're trying to attract them, retain them, and motivate them in our organizations, we need to remember that this generation is not necessarily motivated by money. They are motivated by the experiences they will acquire as part of our team. This may be difficult for us to understand, because previous generations were always thinking, "When am I going to get my next raise? When am I going to get a promotion?" This generation is a little bit different, in that they're more interested in the next exciting opportunity.

I was fortunate enough to be in an intimate session with the author of *The Customer Service Revolution,* Mr. John R. DiJulius. He made a statement that resonates with me every single day. He said, "Don't compete in price wars, compete in experience wars." While he was specifically talking about clients, this quote couldn't be more effective for hiring and retaining millennials. What amazing experiences are we facilitating and creating for our team members?

"As we're trying to attract them, and motivate them we need to remember that this generation is motivated by the experiences they will acquire as part of the team."

In the same manner that Gen Xers place a high value on material things and possessions as a sign of status, millennials place a high value on vacations and life experiences. They use these as a measure of status and success. This is why you will see fewer and fewer millennials buying homes, because they prefer to rent or live at home with their parents much longer. This way, they can use the majority of their income on what they value. Often, unless it's absolutely necessary, millennials will avoid purchasing a car. Again, the value of having a car as a possession is much less than having additional money each month to travel with friends or visit a part of the world they have never seen before.

We must understand this key factor as we build our teams. I will get into more detail in Chapter 5. For now, it's important to note that millennials are more motivated by increasing their experiences than by increasing their pay. That may mean working a ton of hours so that they can take off two weeks to backpack around the world. Or maybe they simply say, "I spend 60 percent of my waking time at a job. It'd better be a great experience." Think about what Google's famous for: their campus lifestyle. People never want to leave work because it's an amazing experience, right? They're probably in a more lavish, fun, and luxurious environment when in the office, than they are when they go home at night. That's why Google is such a magnet for young talent.

Entrepreneurism Is Sexy!

Right now, entrepreneurism is a very hot topic for millennials. Although current studies show that people under the age of 30 are starting businesses at record-low rates, the concept of being an entrepreneur is very attractive to this generation.

We will talk about this more in the next chapter. However, it's important to note that for this millennial generation, there is a big difference between being an entrepreneur and starting a business. For previous generations, these two terms were almost synonymous. But during the last decade, the start-up culture became very popular. Millennials grew up hearing stories about companies such as Facebook, Tesla, and Google. Each of these brand-new "nobody" companies exploded into a dominating force in their markets. These fresh-faced companies took over marketplaces that had been dominated by companies in business for fifty or a hundred years. Millennials saw that being an entrepreneur was the hot, sexy thing, and it was something that they wanted to be "when they grew up."

This generation is not necessarily motivated by traditional, stable jobs that previous generations wanted. Millennials are motivated by the successes of entrepreneurs— the companies and the people in the limelight, on the news, and in the blogs. Young entrepreneurs were having massive success, so this generation grew up motivated and believing that entrepreneurism is the future.

If you were a young adult in the sixties and the seventies, you probably couldn't have named a single billionaire, except for maybe Sam Walton. All of the mega-wealthy, successful people were uncool and much older. You thought you had to spend your entire life trying to accumulate a fortune.

Now fast-forward to the last ten or fifteen years. You've got people in their thirties becoming billionaires like it's a normal thing, thanks to Zuckerberg, Musk, and the people from Google. Millennials see people their age creating amazing empires, so of course they think it's possible for them, too. Think back to when nobody could break the four-minute mile. Roger Bannister finally did it, and then right after that, six other people came up and broke right through his record. Once you know it's possible, that changes the expectations.

Media has created a celebrity status around these successful entrepreneurs. The Gen X teens looked up to and followed musicians. Everyone who was anti-establishment was cool. Now, the exact opposite is true: the people creating the establishment are the celebrities. It's amazing how much has changed with just one generation.

Personal and Work Life Intertwined

The millennial generation blended their personal lives and careers and they want it that way. We talked a little bit earlier about the culture at Google, where employees love work and the environment so much they don't want to leave it. They are comfortable sticking around after their work hours. Sometimes, the lifestyle at work is a better than what they have waiting at home. This generation has closed the gap between personal and work life.

Previous generations like Gen X and Baby Boomers were all about, "I've got to put in my forty hours, and clock out at five o'clock on the dot. When I leave, I'm completely disconnected from work. I don't want anything to do with it, because now it's time to live my life at home and be a mom or dad, or brother or sister, and I want nothing to do with work until Monday at nine in the morning." Millennials are quite the opposite.

> **"Millennials want to love being at work just as much as they love being at home."**

Knowing that this generation builds their work life intertwined with their personal life, we see that millennials want to have their coworkers as their friends. They want to do offsite activities together—hang out on the weekend with their colleagues, talk about their personal lives in the office. It's almost a default for them: they grew up with their friends in school and then they went to college or university together. They're very involved and connected between technology and social media so staying in contact is easy. This generation equates connections on social media as "staying in contact," not necessarily regular phone calls or meaningful chats. They don't have this big differentiation between "Let's turn off and be at home" and "Let's turn on when we're at work." Millennials view the two worlds together; for them, it's almost one thing. They want to love being at work just as much as they love being at home.

This approach ties back into the experiences we've just covered. Thought leaders of this generation like Tim Ferriss and The 4-Hour Workweek, influence millennials to reject the typical career timeline. Older generations were told that they would work hard for a substantial chunk of their lives, and then at the end there's a payoff. The Gen Xer bought into the idea of sweat equity; it's all about work, work, work, and later on in life, you'll be able to reap the benefits. Millennials don't want to work thirty years to reap the benefits. They watched their parents dedicate twenty or thirty years to a company, and then all of a sudden there was some downsizing, and their parents got laid off. Millennials say, "I don't want that to happen to me."

They've seen too many of their parents die young or not ever have the opportunity to enjoy their lives. So, millennials want to enjoy it today. I think there's a real zest for life, and that's generally a good thing. It can be tough to accept thisconcept, though, if you're running your company around the idea that they should be putting in the time and paying their dues today.

Contrast that with a company like VaynerMedia. Gary Vaynerchuk's company is the hottest agency in the country, and everybody's talking about it. They're growing over $100 million in revenue and showing no signs of stopping. I have a friend who worked there and he said they've designed this way: the young generation comes to work and stays after hours, because it's more fun to be there in the office—talking to their friends and working on these mega-celebrity projects—than it is to go to the bar for happy hour. My friend tells me, "It's really hard to ever get out of there. You think the workday's kind of winding down but more people are still coming to the office and the energy level's going up. The next thing you know, you look at the clock, and it's ten thirty at night. You say, 'Oh my gosh, I've got to get out of here—my wife's going to kill me.'" Look at the benefits that organization is reaping, by simply designing their workplace environment to take advantage of the lifestyle that millennials are craving.

Millennials want to love what they do, and they're seeking a career that gives them that. They want to be happy at work, and they want to build friendships there. They don't want to feel like its work; they want to enjoy the process. "I want to work today and go on vacation next week, and then come back and work again."

"Employers who offer unlimited vacations have employees who take very little vacation. The workers feel the purpose in their jobs and never really want to leave."

To take that a step further, it's a big trend today for companies following the lead of Netflix and Google, where there is no set amount of vacation time. It's unlimited vacation time. When someone suggests this, you can see business leaders and other entrepreneurs respond with horror. They think, "My people would never come to work!" But I find employers who offer this perk have employees who take very little vacation. They designed jobs that people love. The workers identify with their job, feel the purpose in it and never really want to leave. Eventually they do want to travel, but they often take less and less vacation because they're so fulfilled by the work they're doing. It's such a win-win for everyone.

Extremely Tech Dependent

One great millennial trait that we can take advantage of right away is that there's no need to train them in technology. We touched on this a little bit while explaining the rest of their characteristics: millennials are very tech dependent.

This generation grew up with computers, gadgets, and gizmos. They are extremely skilled in technology and leverage it naturally. Previous generations often failed to fully utilize technology because they didn't want to adopt new things. Older generations can be set in their ways, wanting to do it the way things have always been done. Most millennials have never used a typewriter, but they grew up using Microsoft Office products like Word and Excel from as early as elementary school. It was expected of them. Although Gen X would include these as skills on their resume, using Word and Excel is second nature to millennials and they see it as general knowledge.

This generation leverages technology in their day-to-day dealings with their friends and family. They know social media inside and out and are comfortable with it. They have the latest and greatest phones, iPods, and tablets—not because they care for them as a material possession—but because the newest technology allows them to leverage on a greater scale. On the flip side, the absence of technology will seriously irritate a millennial. If there's a work environment that does not embrace technology as much as it should, they're not going to be as happy working there.

They can add so much value to a workplace if the company's open to new, innovative ideas on how to do things. Millennials can leverage technology in a way that the company may not have considered, maybe even introducing new, just-released programs. Millennials are on top of the latest and greatest. They are extremely tech dependent, and they are not afraid or embarrassed to share it with you.

"Millennials can revolutionize your business if you'll listen to their ideas."

I think it's common that a younger team member can join a company, take a look at how people are doing things, and say, "Did you guys know there's an app for that?" Or, "If we did this digitally instead of manually, you would cut the cost in half, and it would be done in a fraction of the time." They can revolutionize your business if you'll listen to their ideas. As leaders, we are challenged to keep up and invest in learning these things, because it's going to be hard to lead this generation when they're, at times, thinking ahead of you. They're moving so much faster because they have all these tools at their disposal, and they know how to leverage them.

So, you have the foundation to understand the main characteristics of a millennial. And you realize how their life experiences created these traits. Now, let's use this understanding to give millennials what they are really hoping for and expecting from the workplace, so you can take advantage of their strengths.

CHAPTER 1 RECAP: UNDERSTANDING MILLENNIALS

- Participation was enough. However, without winners or losers, millennials become better team players.
- Music is an integral part of their life so music in the workplace is inviting to them.
- They are highly accustomed to instant gratification; let them innovate your company with processes that bring faster results.
- Helicopter parents impacted their development, blurring the lines of authority. Don't take their questioning as rude or a rejection of authority but understand it's their way of assimilating information.
- Millennials are typically optimistic. Infuse your business with this optimism.
- They prefer experiences over possessions, so entice workers with exciting work environment and experiences, more than with financial motivations.
- Entrepreneurism is sexy to this generation so they dream big and imagine they can conquer the impossible.

- Personal and work life are often intertwined so an attractive work environment offers motivation to enjoy work.
- They are extremely tech dependent and can make your business faster and more cost effective as they introduce tech to the workplace.

For additional details on the characteristics of millennials and to watch quick videos that dive deeper into each of these, please visit my website: www.MeetJavierMontes.com

CHAPTER 2

WHAT DO MILLENNIALS WANT IN THE WORKPLACE?

I SEE SEVEN primary attributes that millennials seek from the workplace. When you satisfy these needs, you'll gain strong millennial workers and diminish the "problems" associated with this age group.

1. Give my work meaning and value
2. Acknowledge my strengths and successes
3. Provide mentorship and training
4. Build a team-oriented and collaborative work environment
5. Let me have fun
6. Provide leadership, not management
7. Encourage an entrepreneurial spirit

Now, let's examine each of these concepts further.

1. GIVE MY WORK MEANING AND VALUE

The first thing that millennials want from their workplace is a job that holds meaning and value. This generation is huge on purpose. They need to understand the why behind the work.

When choosing a place to work, millennials instinctively check your organization's core purpose and they compare it to their personal life purpose. If a millennial feels that the two are congruent, they will the open position. Many organizations fail to clearly state their company's reason for existence; its purpose. To attract millennials, be sure a short statement of purpose is clearly listed on your website and on almost all of your collateral communications. Make sure this is an accurate reflection of your company's purpose. A "bait and switch" where the spoken values are not the true values, will benefit no one. We will talk about articulating company values in Chapter 3.

Additionally, this generation feels passionately about giving back to humanity. They believe: "My efforts have an impact, not only on what I do today, but on the future of the planet, of the world, of the economy." They want to feel like their work has a broad and positive effect. This desire for impact may hold the most weight as they seek:

- A place to work
- A company to represent
- A role
- A career path for the long-term

I have seen it again and again. When millennials ask me for advice on their next step, professionally, they say things like, "Here, I'm really going to have an impact," or, "These guys are doing such great things, and I want to be a part of it." I don't hear them talk about a career ladder. Millennials crave that impact; they want real meaning for their work.

My business field is entertainment. We do luxury musical entertainment for private and corporate events. A lot of people might think, "How does this company create meaning and value? He's not saving the environment." Look below the surface. All of our amazing clients are celebrating something great. They are getting married or celebrating a milestone.

When people consider doing business with us, they're excited. They're ready to get married, they're about to celebrate a birthday, or they want to acknowledge an accomplishment within their company. Every time, they are very excited, and when they're done working with us, they are probably ten times more excited because we gave them the experience of a lifetime.

When people are considering joining our team, one of the things that they are most passionate and fired up about is helping people realize their dream celebrations. A wedding is one of the most important days in some people's lives. That makes it that much more important for my team, because we get to be a part of that dream. We build memories that last a lifetime and our clients are forever grateful to us for bringing their visions to life. Some women imagined their dream wedding from the time they were little girls—my company gets to be a part of that. My team gets to put it all together and it's really exciting for everyone! I think that gives each person on my team a huge sense of purpose, value, and meaning. This is the purpose that attracts them to work for our company and join our team.

"To lead millennials, you need to teach through example."

To lead millennials, you need to teach through example. If your attitude about the company is that you're in it for the money, your workers will not catch the broader vision. Your attitude and mind-set about the company core concept will either attract or repel the top talent that your business deserves.

A fellow entrepreneur and close friend, Jeremy Pound, runs a very successful Internet marketing agency in South Florida named Juicy Results™. He talked about his company's purpose:

> We don't just create marketing here. We are trying to grow businesses—the businesses that have an impact on our community. If we can double the size of a great business, we can create more jobs. Those are also the people who sponsor the little league teams in our communities. Eventually, the really

successful ones also fund the new libraries and the parks and donate to universities. I really sell the vision that by coming to work here, you are participating in the richest part of the American fabric— these small, fast-growing businesses that create value and directly impact our local community.

Amazing! Doesn't it make you feel like your work would have meaning and value? Work to articulate what your company does to bring value, and worry less about awards, rankings, or designs, which carry little-to-no weight with millennials. Create a clear and focused company purpose and then communicate that purpose every opportunity you get.

2. ACKNOWLEDGE MY STRENGTHS AND SUCCESSES

Millennials appreciate having their strengths and successes acknowledged in the workplace.

They love praise and recognition. They want to know the company appreciates their strengths and sees their dedicated time, energy, and effort are adding value to the company. This generation wants you to understand their value and match their strengths to best enhance your business—that they are making a genuine difference.

With that said, millennials are not typically interested in fixing or improving their weaknesses. This generation prefers to focus your attention on their strengths, and even draw your eye away from the areas where they could use more work.

To better understand this millennial mind-set, consider an American football team. An amazing quarterback can throw a great ball, make smooth passes, and insure he gets the ball to the right place at the right time. Those are this quarterback's strengths. He may fall short in blocking, running fast, or catching the ball. So, how does this tie in to millennials? Often corporations say, "Let's improve our team by helping them strengthen their weaknesses. Let's spend all of our time and capital on that."

If you have an amazing quarterback, though, why would you spend time training him to be an amazing receiver? Just because he has weaknesses, doesn't mean that his strengths aren't exactly where they're needed. If your quarterback excels at his position, does he really need to work on those other positions, too? That is exactly how this generation thinks. You're not going to cut your star quarterback because he isn't great at tackling, are you? Of course not. You're going to say, "Let's not ask him to tackle anymore. Let's just keep having him throw the ball." Millennials feel this way. They say, "I know I'm good at x, y, and z. I want a company who recognizes what I can contribute, and will best use my strengths to build their company."

"Millennials want to be recognized, acknowledged, and to know that because of their strengths, the company is moving forward and accomplishing its goals."

Then, once they find a company to capitalize on their strengths and see their accomplishments benefiting the workplace, they want their successes acknowledged. They desire— and even expect— praise each time they have any measure of success. Millennials want to be recognized, acknowledged, and to know that because of their strengths, the company is moving forward and accomplishing its goals. They don't want to feel like an underutilized serf in a seat.

Millennials often ask themselves before accepting a position, "Can my strengths benefit the growth of this company?" The answer to that question determines whether they decide to move forward in a certain workplace.

Just because millennials want their strengths to be front and center doesn't mean they don't want to learn and grow. In fact, this is their next "need."

3. PROVIDE MENTORSHIP AND TRAINING

Millennials naturally have a thirst for learning and they seek it in mentoring and training within their careers.

Although millennials are very aware of their personal weaknesses, they are not necessarily concerned with fixing them. They are more motivated by learning new skills, strengthening their current abilities, and developing new talents. They don't want to be constantly drilled on their shortcomings, but would rather grow new strengths to compensate.

Millennials seek a place where they can learn new skills and new ideas, and where there's somebody to coach, mentor, and train them. Please don't give them a book and tell them, "Here, figure it out." They need one-on-one, back-and-forth communication so they can ask why, gain better understanding, and build new strengths. They want to build a skillset they can take with them throughout their career. These strengths can't be taken away. They are guaranteed to stay with the millennial for this job, and for every job in the future.

This is a critical point. Currently, many companies fail to give their team this kind of training. They bring in an employee, put them through a quick, impersonalized training, and let them loose. Millennials don't want this. They want "coaching." They want a mentor at the company who's going to walk them through, helping them to improve and learn new skills. As part of their entrepreneurial spirit, this generation is not content standing still in terms of their learning. They want to be coached and trained, and they want to know that their company is behind them and is committed to helping them learn new skills.

4. A TEAM-ORIENTED AND COLLABORATIVE WORK ENVIRONMENT

Millennials need to feel like their work has meaning. Part of that comes from being part of something that's bigger than them. They enjoy belonging to a team that accomplishes incredible feats together, that each individual would never be able to accomplish alone. Millennials want a work environment where everybody works together. This is vastly different from previous generations where big business stuck everybody in cubicles. They didn't let workers talk to each other so that they could stay focused and get more work done without distractions. It was a mind-set where distractions equaled less work accomplished and isolation produced more focus and more work. The message: "Get your work done. Crunch numbers for eight hours. Then you can go home."

That is the exact opposite of what this generation is looking for. This generation wants to build their teams. They want to get together, come up with ideas, and explore new options. Millennials want the opportunity to be innovative and collaborate together. They grew up going to school with constant group projects. Starting in middle school, every class had a group project. They were required to work with their peers and they became comfortable with it. They learned that a team can accomplish more than an individual can, and they are looking for the same type of environment when they decide on a workplace.

> **"A team-oriented and collaborative work environment is critical for millennials in the workplace."**

This comes back to the start-up culture. Look at Google and Facebook and see how their offices are laid out, the way they have break rooms, and how everybody works together. This is a break from the hierarchy culture that has existed in big business for decades. Millennials want access to top management. They say, "I want to know I can access the top— or at least higher levels of authority— quickly, without any barriers, or leaders separated on a different floor." They say, "I want to know my voice is being heard." This all comes from being part of this bigger team, this huge conglomerate that's accomplishing the craziest milestones that they could never accomplish on their own. They want to know they have the full support of the entire team, and everybody's backing them. When the team wins a huge success, they want recognition for themselves and the team. A team-oriented and collaborative work environment is critical for millennials in the workplace.

5. Let Me Have Fun

Can't we admit that we all want to have fun? But none want it more than millennials. It's an essential characteristic they look for when deciding on a place to work. They want to have a lot of fun, and it comes in two ways. One is naturally enjoying what they're doing. Two is doing things that are fun and exciting for them.

Millennials expect to enjoy their work life. Unlike Gen Xers, who were always chasing money to buy material possessions, millennials value their experiences. Their time at work is nothing short of another experience for millennials. If they are not enjoying their work and having fun, millennials have no problem resigning their position to go look for something else. Remember, that for millennials, their work life and personal life are completely intertwined. In essence, their personal life is their entire life. Work is just another part of their personal life. Millennials will not live in a constant state of unhappiness at work.

"Millennials expect to enjoy life. Their work life and personal life are completely intertwined so that means work must be fun, too."

They don't want to feel like work is a burden to be endured before they can go off to have fun. They want both things to be mashed up in the workplace. Unfortunately, typical corporate America doesn't understand this concept. Most companies like to be very strict on work time and set harsh company policies, like not allowing access to social media during work hours. In some companies, cell phones are not allowed to be on while at work. That's the opposite of what millennials want. Millennials want to enjoy what they do. They want to do it with people around them whom they enjoy being with, and they want to do it in a way they consider fun so it doesn't feel like "work."

Incorporating fun into the workplace isn't difficult, but it will take some effort. In my company, birthdays are a big part of our company culture. Birthdays are huge because we take almost an entire day to celebrate the birthday of a team member. It starts with a surprise welcoming for that member when he/she arrives at the office. They are greeted with loud music and cheers from the rest of the team. Next, we bring out a small cake and sing "Happy Birthday." The team typically decorates their desk with balloons and streamers, and gives them a personalized card signed by every team member. Then we typically go off-site for a lunch and some kind of fun activity—like bowling. We surprised one person with a celebration a week early. We typically try to catch them off guard and that makes for especially fun memories.

Our company meetings offer another example. Most people dread corporate/department meetings. Here at EMG, we inject fun while still sticking to the agenda. One part of the meeting invites participants to recognize someone for exemplifying our company's core values (more on core values in Chapter 3). We have a small basketball hoop in the conference room. The person recognized for living the core value gets to stand up and take a shot at the basketball hoop. If they make it, they are rewarded with a ten-dollar gas card. It's always fun and exciting, and everyone cheers during basketball time!

Organizing and incorporating fun into your company culture is not a complex task, but it does require work and effort. It needs to come from the leader—the CEO, the manager of the department, or somebody who's in a leadership position. As this culture evolves in your organization, the group will start to develop leaders who will take on this concept and execute it better than the business owner or CEO. Your team will start to naturally put these things together.

When we first started celebrating birthdays, I had to personally initiate it and come up with all the ideas and execution. I found it a little tough to try to come up with all these things and be creative with all of it. At first, I almost felt like I was pushing this onto the team. But it became easier as some people on my team were more creative than I. They executed much better than I could... and more important, they enjoy doing it much more than I did.

What I am describing is not business-as-usual for most companies. It probably requires a mind shift for many organizations. It's very different. But in my experience, it has always yielded extremely positive results.

6. Provide Leadership, Not Management

How do we run a business without managing our people? I want to start off by saying that I am not suggesting that you do not manage your team. I am simply saying that the style of management needs to be a bit different from what has been traditionally accepted.

To attract millennials, entrepreneurs, business owners, and CEOs need to change our management style away from the ones with which we are currently comfortable. To successfully lead millennials, we need to own the role as the visionary and entrepreneur of the organization. Millennials want someone they can look up to and someone they can follow. This style focuses on leadership— showing the way, rather than management— telling the way. Remember that millennials have a knack for questioning authority. When authority isn't there or doesn't push back that's not a problem. So in order to bypass the adversarial role that could occur, millennials need to be inspired and motivated by somebody who leads by example and frees them to explore. Management cannot micromanage. Millennials hate it. Again, this is the generation that goes on the Internet and googles all the answers. They want to choose to follow somebody who's been there and done that, and from whom they can learn.

"This generation wants to follow somebody who has dreams that are bigger than themselves, who is optimistic and positive."

New members who join your team will watch the leaders in your company. They're going to mimic what the leaders do because they look up to them and want to see the same results. Again, as you're building your team or your department, it's critical that you pick the right people to be on your team. You don't want people following the wrong leader or mimicking the wrong activities or behaviors.

A great leader gives recognition to his team whenever it's due. A great leader will give praise as often as possible. This is one of the seven characteristics that motivate and inspire millennials. This generation wants to follow somebody who has dreams that are bigger than themselves. They are motivated by a leader who has the mind-set of, "The sky's the limit, and we can accomplish anything." They want to follow somebody who's extremely optimistic about life and who's always emitting positive energy.

As you begin to develop teams, ask, "Am I that leader?" Richard Branson constantly talks about himself as the cheerleader of Virgin. That's a perfect example of where we need to be as the leaders of our organizations. Most managers today spend their time looking at reports and numbers, telling their direct employees what to do, and pretending to run successful meetings. Millennials look at that kind of leader and say, "I don't want to be like that!" To be a successful leader of millennials, we should lead by example and set the trend for the rest of our team to follow in actions and decisions.

This is a philosophy that Jack Welch, CEO of GE and founder of the Jack Welch Management Institute, has preached for years. He says that he wants his top people to lead, not manage. "Managers control, they don't facilitate," says Welch. "Managers complicate things, they don't simplify them. Managers keep their feet on the brakes, in a manner of speaking, rather than on the gas."

Managers are people who can read reports, enforce key performance indicators (KPIs), and enforce rules. A leader can do those things, but in a way where they lead by example—and they motivate others to follow them. They inspire people to do the best that they can do. In today's competitive business environment, we need to develop leaders in our organizations. This is exactly what the millennial generation is seeking from the companies for which they choose to work.

It's still important to manage our people's output, but we want to do it in a way where they're inspired and growing as individuals.

7. Encourage an Entrepreneurial Spirit

Millennials naturally have this entrepreneurial spirit inside of them and they look for that in the workplace as well. Now more than ever, start-ups and companies are emerging out of nowhere and exploding on the scene. Millennials see people their age growing these companies and having massive success. This is the sexiest profession in the world right now. Millennials want to be part of companies that:

- Experience exponential growth
- Want to take risks
- Innovate new things
- Bring new products to their market
- Bring new ideas and inventions to the world

They want to be part of a team that disrupts traditional ways of doing things. The ironic part of this is that millennials do not want to necessarily own their own businesses. This is a neat concept because when you talk to millennials, they have a very different definition of entrepreneurship than the one we are used to. According to a recent study, "Millennials and the Future of Work" from oDesk and Millennial Branding, about 90 percent of millennials think of entrepreneurship, not necessarily as starting one's own business, but as having a risk-taking and self-starting mind-set, and as someone who can identify opportunities. That's a different definition than what we've used in the business world for decades, but that is how millennials view entrepreneurship. Ironically, 60 percent of millennials consider themselves entrepreneurs, which is even crazier! They don't own their businesses, but they consider themselves entrepreneurs. Another cool statistic is that 67 percent of millennial employees would leave their current jobs right now for a more creative and self-employed opportunity. That's two-thirds of millennials who are currently employed right now said they would actually leave their jobs for an opportunity like that.

"Millennials think of entrepreneurship not necessarily as starting one's own business, but as having a risk-taking and self-starting mind-set, and as someone who can identify opportunities."

How can we capitalize on that in our company? We should share our experiences and teach millennials how we run our business. Teach your team how the business makes money, how the business loses money, and how it generates profits. They want to learn about these things. Millennials want to have information. They feel a need to have the inside scoop on the company they work with. And they can use this information to better understand how they can add to the success of the company.

This is a great opportunity for companies because business is cool. Back in the eighties, Gen X was motivated by all the musicians and MTV. We are fortunate. Millennials actually look up to businesspeople and entrepreneurs as today's stars. Business is a good thing; being productive is fun. We should be taking advantage of this to grow our teams because we can have really motivated people; people who are looking to be part of an organization for which they can be passionate.

Millennials want to contribute to the success of your company now and in the future. Again, their entrepreneur spirit invites them to enjoy work with meaning and impact. They can't get motivated by a company that stagnates. They don't want to join a company that doesn't have a long-term vision. They avoid companies satisfied with a 5 percent growth per year. The average and normal doesn't motivate or excite millennials.

They want a company that is optimistic, has unrealistic goals that just blows their mind, and that goes out and executes and makes those things happen. This is what drives them and ignites their internal fire. This is how they consider themselves successful; this fuels their engine. Millennials have the same entrepreneur spirit that most small business owners have within them. Sometimes they don't know how to explain it or put that into words for us to understand, but it's there. We simply need to know how to capitalize on that and leverage it in our organizations.

Time and time again, significance has been proven to be an important factor in being happy in the workplace—something that people desire, need, and crave. It's extremely important for mental health and emotional health in humans of all ages. I think that it transcends the millennials. What's different is that millennials are very comfortable identifying these needs and then going out and seeking their significance from their workplace. If we can successfully align a millennial's passion and purpose with our organization's focus and values, we'll gain a more engaged employee and find greater success and momentum in the company.

CHAPTER 2 RECAP: WHAT DO MILLENNIALS WANT IN THE WORKPLACE?

- Be clear about the "why" behind the work so millennials can understand and see that their work has meaning and value.
- Acknowledge their strengths and successes and allow them to build on their strengths... not spend time trying to improve their weaknesses.
- Provide mentorship and training one-on-one so millennials can learn new ideas and new skills.
- Build a team-oriented and collaborative work environment where millennials can feel the excitement of being part of something bigger than themselves.
- Create fun in your work environment so millennials can enjoy their combined life/work.
- Provide leaders millennials want to look up to and follow, not management that directs them in what to do.
- Encourage an entrepreneurial spirit that invites them to seek opportunities, innovate, and use their talents and creativity.

For the most up-to-date material and additional information on millennials and to watch quick videos that dive deeper into these concepts, please visit my website: www.MeetJavierMontes.com

CHAPTER 3

COMPANY CULTURE FOR MILLENNIALS

NOW THAT WE understand the millennial mind-set, and we know what they want in the workplace, we can talk about actionable steps to create an ecosystem within our organization where millennials can thrive. We'll discuss how to design our companies from a philosophical level, as well as from a tangible level. The first thing in our organization that we must look at is our current office culture.

It seems that every business book makes some reference to having a healthy culture in your organization. It's an imperative item to the success of your business. Jack Daly (Hyper Sales Growth), Cameron Herold (Double Double), Verne Harnish (Mastering the Rockefeller Habits), and every other expert in the business world will tell you that without the right company culture in place, it is virtually impossible for your organization to succeed. The question is not whether your company has a culture. Whether you like it or not, your company has its own culture right now. The important question to ask yourself is, "Has this culture been created by design, or by default?" All of your employees today are contributing to your culture and are directly affected by it every day. This couldn't be more true for millennials.

CORE VALUES

A company culture is typically not easily described in a few words or phrases; it's usually something that can be felt and sensed in the air as soon as you walk into any company. Unfortunately, millennials are not the best at taking subtle hints. If you want to catch a millennial's attention with your culture, you will need to put some serious effort into making your company culture come vibrantly alive in your workplace. Millennials need this office culture to be obvious and bright in order for them to wholeheartedly feel like your organization could be a home for them.

The first step to creating your company culture, or bringing your current culture to life, is to establish your company's core values. What exactly are core values? The core values of your company are a set of ideas, principles, or concepts that dictate behavior and action for your organization. They help you clearly understand and define what is right and what is wrong. It may be hard to identify these values because they are so close and innate to the way that your company naturally behaves—they seem a natural part of your environment. Your company's core values are engrained in the way that your team thinks, talks, celebrates, eats, and drinks.

Core values really emerge from the business owner, CEO, or executive team. If you're a small business, with only a few employees or maybe just yourself, your core values are very similar to (if not exactly) what your personal core values are. If you're a much larger organization, then maybe it's a combination of the personal core values of your executive team and the top employees in your company. Once you have defined and implemented your company's core values throughout your team, you will soon discover that these core values are the glue that holds your team together. If you don't identify core values, you will constantly wonder why certain people fit well within your team and others seem to stick out like sore thumbs. These are the values that you naturally hold near and dear to you, and they are the most important concepts for all decision-making in your company.

Your articulated set of values needs to be extremely clear and concise and it should be incorporated in all aspects of your business. If your business does not have core values, now is a good opportunity to take some time to work on identifying and establishing your core values. There are plenty of good books and content on the Internet that can help you with this process, but the main resource that I used for my company was the book *Mastering the Rockefeller Habits* by Verne Harnish.

Once you have your core values established, the next step comes down to bringing those core values to life in your office culture. This is the step where 95 percent of organizations fail miserably. Most organizations invest the time to establish some great company values, but they don't take the time and effort to implement them in their organization's culture. They don't make the core values active and vibrant in the organization. For example, in our business, not one hour goes by at the office where, at some level and at some conversation, the core values are not mentioned. Because they set the stage for your organization's company culture, they need to permeate your workplace in order for millennials (and your entire team in general) to truly understand and embrace your core values.

Core values should be evident everywhere in your organization. At EMG, our core values are listed in a large frame on the wall, on our website, in the employee manuals, and even on all of our job opening postings. Our core values are incorporated in every daily, weekly, monthly, quarterly, and yearly meeting. Our core values are brought to life by our systems and processes, and they help us recognize each other's successes because we can always tie them back to one or more of our core values. It drives everything we do and every decision we make.

You can even list them on your team's business cards. Everywhere that people come across your organization, they should know what your core values are. This will lay the foundation for your team, internally, and it will slowly make its way into attracting your ideal customers and ideal suppliers, who will live by the same or similar core values. Core values also present an amazing opportunity to scale your company. As your business grows, every decision you make needs to run a litmus test past your core values. If it's in line with your core values, then you can proceed. If it's not, then you know very quickly that it's not where your organization should be heading. This also empowers your team to make decisions. It provides them a clear and easy way to know that they are making the right decision without needing to receive a final blessing from you or appropriate management.

HIRING BASED ON CORE VALUES

After bringing your core values to life in your organization, it's time to walk the walk. It's time to begin making hiring decisions based on your company's core values. By implementing this concept, you will soon build an entire organization of people who believe in and live by the same core values. This is a marked change from the way most organizations hire.

Most companies are conditioned to make hiring decisions solely based on a candidate's skill set and experience. Having a perfect skill set and experience match for your current open position seems like the logical choice. But many case studies, many personal experiences, and many business books will prove that if a person is not a good cultural fit for your organization, it does not matter how amazing his/her skill set is. This person will not last very long in your organization. That person will cause a lot of unnecessary stress and conflict among your team, not participate, and not work well with your team. They may flat out quit because they are truly unhappy at your organization. Therefore, all the time and money spent bringing this person into your company, training them on your internal systems and processes, and dealing with the internal issues they caused as a wrong cultural fit will be a complete waste of resources. Then you will realize that bringing in an "amazing skill set", absent of your core values was actually a liability for your company, not an asset.

Like many of you reading this book, I was skeptical about implementing this in my company. However I decided to try it after hearing this concept so many times from respected business leaders and seeing the massive evidence they presented. When I finally took the leap and changed my hiring method, I can wholeheartedly say it drastically changed my business! This simple concept changed my business 180 degrees. There is so much power in having new hires "just get it." The learning curve is so much shorter; they are almost immediately accepted by the rest of your team. They think and act like you, so you can quickly feel confident enough to let them make decisions on their own because they will be almost the exact same decisions that you would have made.

For years I had struggled to find a way to teach new hires how to think and act as I would. It was one of the most frustrating things for me, because I was trying to scale my business. I was limited by my employees because they couldn't make the right decisions while fulfilling their responsibilities. I had to have every decisions run by me first to avoid possible damage to our company. This is no way to run or scale a business. And it's definitely a formula for personal burnout. If I couldn't empower my team to own their roles and make decisions— because they'd be wrong— then why did I even have a team?

Today, we hire 100 percent based on our company core values. We will hire people who are a perfect culture fit, not people who have the right skill set for the open position. In fact, for most positions, we hire candidates who have no skill set for the open position but are impeccable culture fits, as long as they have the drive and ambition to learn and excel. That's how much we value having the right people on our team. I have even found people I knew I wanted to hire— even though I had no idea what position I would hire them for— solely because they were perfect for our culture.

The beginning is the hardest part of implementing this in your organization. Any major change in a business can be challenging and frustrating at first, especially if you want to fill a position quickly. The problem is, more than 90 percent of the people who apply for a position at your company are not going to be a good culture fit. People may have an amazing resume, they may have amazing skills, and they may blow you away with a lot of other things—but their mind-set does not fit well with your team.

"As leaders of our organizations, one of the biggest roles and responsibilities we have is to protect our culture."

As leaders of our organizations, one of the biggest roles and responsibilities we have is to protect our culture. You protect that culture by making sure the people on your team, the people you bring on, and the people you retain in your company are good culture fits for your organization. Without that, you can destroy everything you have built, regardless of how long you have been in business. The people on your team who are the right culture fit are going to start to feel awkward if you allow somebody who's not a good culture fit to come into your company. If you keep this bad fit in your company long enough, you will see your good fits consider leaving your company—and your bad fits will do the same because they are unhappy and stick out like sore thumbs on your team. Then you'll be left with two or more open seats in your company because you filled one open seat with a bad apple. It's a scenario that I have seen happen far too many times and it becomes a lose-lose for everyone involved.

After experiencing first-hand the power and effect of this concept on my business, I'm convinced this is how every business should hire. Even though this method has become more popular recently, I still see many entrepreneurs and large organizations struggling with this. Although it is a simple process, it is by no means easy.

People say, "How do I screen for culture? How do I get this right? How do I make sure that they're a good culture fit before actually giving them the opportunity to work for me?" I have developed a rock-solid hiring process I use, which I detail for you in Chapter 7. You can use it to immediately start hiring correctly. For this chapter, we need to understand that in order to fully develop our company culture and bring it to life, we need to have an entire team of people who think and act by the same values as your organization. To accomplish that, it starts by allowing only the correct individuals to join your team's culture.

Firing Based on Core Values

The next step to getting your entire team aligned with your company culture is to implement a new standard in your company. You'll need to remove people from your team who don't live by the same values as your company. In this section, we will cover why it is essential that your core values are extremely clear to all members of your team.

Keep in mind this phrase: "Culture is defined by what you reward and what you tolerate." Your entire team is looking at you every day. They're taking mental notes of those things that you're rewarding, and they're noticing all of the things that you're tolerating. As much as you would like to think that your team will not do things that you don't like, they will keep doing them as long as you keep tolerating them. This is another example of not just talking the talk, but walking the walk. As you let things slide, you are adding to the creation of your organization's culture. On the flip side, when you absolutely do not tolerate something, that also adds to your culture. Are the rules you put in place meant to be followed all the time, or do you allow them to be followed only sometimes? Do your rules apply equally to every member on your team, or are some members allowed to routinely break certain rules?

> **"There are no warnings, no write-ups, and no three-strike rule for violating any of our core company values. A violation of any core value at any time during employment equals immediate termination."**

In our company—and it should be this way for all companies—core values are nonnegotiable items. If somebody on my team violates any one of our core values, it is immediate grounds for termination. My entire team knows this. In fact, people who are only coming in for an interview are made aware of this. We spend a lot of time explaining to them that they can put up a front to try to make us think that they live by our core values, but if they really don't, then at some point within the first few weeks of employment, we're going to catch on. When we do, it is immediate grounds for termination. There are no warnings, no write-ups, and no three-strike rule for violating any of our core company values. It's a very clear and simple decision. A violation of any one of our core values at any time during employment equals immediate termination. If you expect your team to take your company culture seriously, it starts with the leader fully embracing the fact that a purposely designed company culture is imperative to unify any team that wants to achieve massive results. Any tolerated deviation from that design will eventually be detrimental to the organization and may put its survival at risk.

PURPOSE

Now that you have your core values in place and have begun to use them for some of the most important processes of your organization, the next thing to consider in designing your culture is purpose. What is the core purpose of your company? What are you here for? What are you trying to accomplish? What's the reason why your company exists? What are you trying to change in the world? This is the *why* for your company.

In his book Start with Why, Simon Sinek helps us understand the importance of using our why in business and in our personal lives. His detailed explanation can help you understand how to arrive at your why.

In order to inspire millennials, your company needs to have a very compelling why, or purpose. Millennials are driven by this purpose. Instinctively, millennials choose a company to work for based on whether or not they connect with your company's purpose. Millennials may not be directly looking for a company's purpose as they make a decision on employment, but they will be inherently drawn to it. And they will be much more excited to pursue a path with a company that can clearly and compellingly explain its core purpose. If they can align with your purpose, then they will be very happy within your organization for the long term. When they truly believe in your purpose, they will be extremely motivated and will help you achieve great things.

The biggest problem I see in most businesses today is that companies don't have a clear sense of their purpose. Most entrepreneurs and businesses leaders say something like, "Well, we're just trying to make money." Larger organizations have this concept of a mission or vision statement that's some wordy sentence that sits in a frame in the executive's office. Ironically, most of these executives have no clue what's in those frames. Almost always, these statements are lengthy, wordy and don't really mean a thing. The worst part is that 95 percent of the employees in that company have no idea what these statements are either. Why is that? It's because it doesn't connect with them.

It's not going to connect with millennials either. Millennials have a pretty good sense of what their purpose in life is. They may not be able to verbalize it well when prompted, but they feel it deep inside their hearts and typically make most of their decisions (including career decisions) based on this purpose. Once millennials are exposed to your company's core purpose, they will run their mental test next to it and ask themselves:

"Do I believe that your company can accomplish this, and do I want to be a part of this? If I do, then I have a purpose within your company. My purpose is to help you achieve your purpose. I want to be a part of this organization's purpose, and I want to help propel this organization forward. Therefore, I know that my work has meaning."

If your company's purpose is not defined or is unclear, your organization will fail the millennials' purpose test and they will move on to the next company. Your company will fail to be an option for them because they can't understand your purpose or align their personal purpose with your organization and its purpose.

The main goal for your purpose statement is to make it extremely simple and clear so it can be repeated often. It is an additional tool that leaders should use to make all decisions in the company. Will this decision help us in moving in the direction of achieving our core purpose? Besides new employees, your core purpose will attract the right customers, the right suppliers, and the right investors to your organization. Your company's purpose is another item that should be listed everywhere in your organization: on your website, on your receipts and invoices, on your letterhead, and on your business cards.

All the leaders in the organization should be referencing your core purpose in all meetings, performance reviews, brainstorming sessions, and multiple times throughout the workday. The goal is that all employees and stakeholders of your organization can quickly recite your core purpose with as much ease as they can state the name of your company. Before our leadership team could sit down and work on our company's purpose, we required each member to read the book *Third Circle Theory: Purpose Through Observation* by Pejman Ghadimi. This helped each of us get a clear sense of our own personal purpose and motivation in life, before coming together and realizing how intertwined each of our purposes was rooted within the company. Even if your company does not have a leadership team yet, I would strongly recommend that you read the book before establishing your organization's purpose.

FLEXIBLE WORK HOURS AND LOCATION

The next item to discuss when creating a company culture for millennials is typically the most controversial, and sometimes it's the most difficult to execute successfully. This is the topic of having flexible work hours and flexible work locations.

Naturally, this is also the section that baby boomers and Gen Xers have the hardest time understanding and agreeing to incorporate into their organizations. To be fully transparent, this is an area that I also struggled with in the beginning. In my family's house, we were raised with a standard that we worked from 9:00 a.m. to 5:00 p.m. You clock in; you clock out. You do this every single day. Every now and then, you get a holiday and, after a certain amount of time, you get vacation days. Depending on your tenure, you might get additional time off. That's the way I was raised, so I started my business like that.

I started hearing about this concept of flexible work hours and working from home but I didn't think it would work. As I started the company, I realized that I didn't enjoy having to be there at nine o'clock. Sometimes I was motivated to come in at seven in the morning. Sometimes I wanted to do something else in the morning and I wanted to come in at eleven o'clock and stay later to finish my work for the day. When I started giving myself that flexibility, I realized that I felt happier those days, and I felt more productive with the time I spent at work. I justified this flexibility because I was the owner and the entrepreneur. But I believed I was the only one in my company who would care enough or be disciplined enough to come in late and still make sure that my work was completed before I left. But then I thought, if this is true for me, then it could be true for the rest of my team. By this time, I was pretty confident in my team because I had hired them based on our company core values. And if they were hired based on core values, then my entire team should think and behave the same way I did. If my team could be happier or more comfortable when given the flexibility to decide at what time they wanted to start working, they might enjoy working a little bit more, as opposed to having a dictator saying, "Everybody clocks in at nine. Everybody stays until five."

I pondered this concept and realized if it worked, I could have a happier and more productive team. And that increased productivity could give me a strong competitive advantage over others in my industry. One day,

I took a leap of faith and made the drastic change. I announced to my company that we were no longer going to have set schedules. All team members could come in to work and leave at any time that they chose. However, this came with a caveat: everybody was still responsible for all their work. They could make their schedules as they liked; however, all their deliverables were still going to be required.

This change struck a chord within my company. My team described it as a ton of weight being lifted off their shoulders. They felt an unexplainable sense of freedom they never had before. No longer did they feel uneasy asking to come in a little later because they had to make a medical appointment. No longer did parents feel bad about missing their kids' school awards or plays. I can't even count how many hours of my time I saved myself by eliminating these conversations when people asked to come in later or leave earlier. If you talk to the members of my team, every single one of them will tell you that this is one of the things that they value the most. This is one of the things that actually challenges them to be more productive. Because they value it so much, they don't want to ever lose this privilege. Today in my company, we have absolutely no set schedules; people can come and go as they please. Whatever time you want to come in, and whatever time you want to leave the office, that's up to you. You know what your deliverables are and that is what the rest of the team expects from you.

There are a few times my team is required to be at the office. All team members are required to be present in person at all of our weekly, monthly, and quarterly meetings. For our daily meetings "huddles", our team members have the option to appear by phone. Outside of that, their entire schedule is 100 percent up to them. At first, this concept can be very difficult to get used to, especially if your team is small. There were many mornings that I found it tough to come into the office and find myself the only person there. I'd wait a few hours, and maybe one person would show up. Although it was a difficult pill to swallow, I reminded myself, I was the entrepreneur and I have always been the first one at the office anyways.

The good news is when you start seeing the positive results. The first thing that happens is that your team becomes more productive and you see your production go up. After that, you see your team start caring more about their results as opposed to the amount of time that they've spent at the office. This, after all, is what we care about too!

I drive this concept of flexible hours into my team from day one of the first interview. At first, most candidates get excited and amused by this concept. But after I finish explaining it, everyone feels empowered and challenged. The last catch to our flexible hours environment is tied directly into one of our company core values: have fun. The last catch is that nobody in our company is allowed to work over forty hours in a week—not even me. Now understand, it can be challenging when you need to accomplish all of your KPIs (key performance indicators) for the week, but under no circumstances are you allowed to pass forty hours. During our first interview, we start by explaining that at our company, nobody works more than forty hours per week. Their initial response is typically along the lines of "Okay, that's kind of what I'm used to."

I then go on to say, "No. What you don't understand is that we don't have any set schedules here. You work whenever you want, as often as you want, and as much as you want—so long as you don't work more than forty hours." Why? Because, in our team, our company culture sets the stage that there needs to be a very strong work-life balance. We believe that every person who comes to work at our company should be able to accomplish all the work he needs to accomplish within forty hours. If you cannot complete your work within forty hours, then you are not the right person for our team.

"The irony is that our biggest fear for not starting this system earlier— namely, that people wouldn't ever come in to work—has had the opposite outcome: people actually started working more."

Now, if you want to get all your work done in thirty hours, then that's okay, and highly encouraged. What you are not allowed to do is work forty-one hours, ever. We drive that concept very much, especially because we consider this a violation of one of our core values. And remember, violating a core value is grounds for immediate termination. If people work more than forty hours of work per week our experience shows that will eventually lead to burnout. People get tired and feel like they're working all the time. In the long run, over-work will not give you a good return on your investment.

As leaders, we want our team to be happy. We want them to have this work-life balance. As mentioned before, millennials will intertwine their work and their personal lives. What soon happens is they start working from home. Working from home allows them to easily get carried away and work twelve-hour days, mostly because it doesn't feel like work to them. They enjoy what they're doing and are having fun doing it. They are passionate about working to fulfill their purpose. Before they even realize it, they will find themselves always working. The irony of this story is that our biggest fear for not starting this system earlier—namely, that people wouldn't ever come in to work—has had the opposite outcome: people actually started working more.

There is one very important factor that comes into play when trying to successfully implement this system into an organization. You must make sure that you are fully confident in the way that you are measuring success. Without having this piece in place, the system will be a complete disaster. When you clearly define each person's deliverables and expected results, you can have peace of mind while allowing flexibility. You need to clearly articulate to your team what "getting all your work done" actually means. This is facilitated by establishing a set of KPIs for each role in your company. In our company, we establish a position's KPIs before beginning the recruiting and interview process. Some simple examples of KPIs for a salesperson might be the number of calls made in a day or week. Another KPI might be the number of proposals sent out this week. I will explain this in greater detail in Chapter 6.

In order to successfully implement this system, we must have KPIs in place that will allow us to objectively measure and ensure that each team member is being effective. Most leaders have this misconception of "I need all my employees in the office so I can see them and be sure they're working." But this mind-set wastes time. It's far better to implement systems and processes to effectively measure deliverables in your company. If these leaders had objective data that rated each person in the company on a real-time basis, they would feel extremely confident allowing their teams to create their own schedules. Then they could simply hold them accountable to their own results. This is the tradeoff that allows for this kind of flexibility.

In my company, we use a Customer Relationship Management (CRM) software to track all of our metrics (KPIs) for each member of the team. Everything we do runs through our company's CRM. We have dashboards that give us up-to-the-minute metrics on every single person in the company and their respective roles. Having this extremely powerful tool gives me the confidence as a leader to know that all of the company's production is being met on a daily basis. Without having a tool like this in place, I think it's easy for us to default to that worry of, "Are they actually working?" or "How effective is somebody being?" or "If they're not in the office, then I assume they're not working."

Another widely controversial policy that we have in our company is that everyone gets unlimited time off. You read it right: unlimited! We don't track vacation time. After your first ninety days at EMG, you can take as much vacation time as you want. If you want to disappear for three weeks, go right ahead. Like I said, the caveat is you're responsible to make sure that the work gets done. You're solely responsible to make sure that you're bringing in what you need to bring in for a week, month, quarter, and year. Every single person in my company owns this. Every single person on my team knows how they affect the rest of the team. They know how they contribute to the success of the company. We fully understand that if we don't do our work, the entire company suffers. Therefore, every team member has a personal interest in ensuring that their work is taken care of before considering taking time off.

Before this policy, when somebody asked me to go on vacation, I would be responsible for figuring out who was going to cover for them, answer their phone calls, and respond to their emails. It was a dreadful process. I dreaded every time someone asked me for vacation time.

Today, I don't have these worries. Somebody says, "I'm going to go on vacation for two weeks." I say, "Great. Have fun." They turn around and assign their emails to somebody. They assign somebody to take care of their phone calls and any projects they are working on. They ask others to pick up their slack while they're out for the two weeks. It's not my responsibility anymore. The employees own it because they know how important their roles are. And they know how they are measured. They know if they stop their production and stop what they're doing, it affects the entire team—and ultimately their careers within the company. Once again, it's ironic that since implementing this policy, fewer of my team members actually take vacations. Perhaps it's because the pressure is off of losing unused vacation hours. We are giving them as many as they want, and as often as they want.

This policy is basically creating a checks-and-balances system, giving them the responsibility of coordinating it with their team members. The system is transferring ownership from management to the individual and to the team as a whole. That reduces a lot of stress for leaders and it empowers millennials because they have control.

Allowing your team to work from home or remotely is a concept that gained a lot of traction during the last few years. In his book *The 4-Hour Workweek*, Tim Ferriss shows the possibilities and the mind-set it would take to accomplish our week's work in just four hours. He even lays out a plan to convince your employer to allow you to work from home. As technology continues to improve and companies embrace this concept, allowing your team to partially work from home may become standard practice. Even today, I don't understand how any organization doesn't give a laptop to each employee. Who runs on PC towers anymore? How can you expect your team be tied to a desk? Millennials definitely don't want to be tied to a desk; they want to be on the go. This concept of being able to work remotely is only possible by having your entire team working on laptops, not PC towers.

Even the type of computers that your company chooses to offer plays a part in dictating company culture. If someone sees you offer laptops to your team, you're indirectly sending a message that your company can be mobile and remote, at times. If people see workers in a cubicle with a monitor that they can't take with them, you're sending out a different message. Making decisions like this for your culture is extremely important.

Millennials find other ways to be mobile. One team member liked to work on a PC. One day she was out of the office. All of a sudden, it looked like a ghost took over her computer and started moving things on her screen. The mouse pointer on the screen was moved and clicked on things and was productive, but the physical mouse on her desk did not move at all. All of us at the office were staring and asked, "What is going on?" We asked this person the next day. She said, "I downloaded a program where I can access this computer from my computer at home, and I control it from home. That's how I work."

Millennials don't see boundaries. They find new and interesting ways for our companies to leverage technology. They make things happen. These millennials will always find more innovative and productive ways to get things done. This is the power of having millennials on your team. You'll learn a lot of new things and find ways to be much more effective.

FOSTERING A SENSE OF BELONGING TO A TEAM
THAT IS DOING SOMETHING GREAT

Finally, when developing a company culture that is inspiring and motivating for millennials you want to foster a solid and unified team. As Aristotle once said, "The whole is greater than the sum of its parts." The most important thing to know about a team is that though each of your individuals might be amazing individually, together they are much more powerful and can accomplish exponential results.

Some leaders get stuck on this one and skip this step. They think that their company is too small—or too big—to be able create this feeling in their organization. They think that making a change will be too difficult and arduous a task. Or perhaps they think their ideas seem too small to have any real impact on their organizations and they will go unnoticed and ignored. There are many things that leaders can do to create this environment in today's organizations, but I am going to share one of the simple things that we did in our company that I think all companies should do.

Through the years, our company has developed an extremely tight culture. Like most companies, we spend many hours together every single week. Sometimes we spend more time with our coworkers than we do with our friends and family. A few years back, I decided to make a very small change in the way that I referred to my employees. I started referring to all of our employees as team members or family members. Within a few months, the entire company unconsciously followed suit. We always have such good times together that we don't refer to each other as employees or even coworkers anymore. We talk about each other as team members and even family members. When we talk about our company as EMG, we talk about The EMG Family. We refer to The EMG Team. I think this is an easy, actionable item that all business owners can implement into their organizations tomorrow. Then they will see the ripple effect it has on the team pretty quickly.

You're going to sense that the office culture will naturally come together a lot more. People will grow closer and start working with each other on projects much more fluidly. I think that this small change is an important part of what millennials are looking for when they are choosing a team. They want to belong to a family. They want a sense of the company being a home as opposed to just a workplace. As I mentioned earlier, it all comes full circle in the concept of millennials viewing work life and personal life as one singular thing that's intertwined. Those soft benefits go a long way when it comes to people staying loyal to the team and not taking offers from other companies, even when someone's offering them more money.

Most people naturally want to be part of something that's bigger than themselves. They want to be part of a winning team. They want to be part of a group of people who can achieve something that's bigger than them. They don't want to be another number, and they don't want to be just another employee at just another company. Millennials are extremely aware of this concept and strive to be a valuable part of a company's team.

CHAPTER 3 RECAP: COMPANY CULTURE FOR MILLENNIALS

- Core values come from top leaders and their personal values. Codify these core values.
- Integrate core values into your company culture, printed material, and all meetings to unite millennials and others in purpose, goals, and decision making.
- Hiring based on core values is more successful than hiring based on job skills.
- Living your core values means firing workers who violate them.
- A clear company purpose inspires millennials and insures they are a good fit for you.

- Flexible hours and work location increase production when you also have key performance indicators and accurate CRM tracking metrics.
- Unlimited vacation time empowers millennials and reduces your workload.
- Fostering a sense of team and belonging attracts millennials

Sign up for my weekly video blog that provides some powerful insight into the millennial generation via my website: www.MeetJavierMontes.com

CHAPTER 4

OFFICE LAYOUT

THE OFFICE LAYOUT is extremely important because it's where everything happens. Having a good layout is crucial for maximizing the productivity, collaboration, and job satisfaction of your team.

WHAT I TRIED

I did a few things unintentionally before I found a really good office layout. My first office was small but workable. We had a small waiting room in the front, an adjacent work area, and a room for presentations or meetings. Everybody worked in the work area, except me. As the CEO and "management," I worked in the main presentation area. I met my clients in that area as well. The small team worked in the main work area. It gave me privacy as the manager to meet with people individually and the rest of the team was together where they would collaborate, build things, and get their work done. This worked well—until we started growing.

Now that the budget was a bit bigger we wanted to get everybody into big private offices. Our next office actually had windows in it and everyone had a nice view. Everybody was excited to get a private office, myself included. We had a waiting room, meeting room, break room and a recording studio room— which was great.

When we got into this layout, we thought that this was the best. This was what we'd been working for, and everybody was excited about it.

People got to decorate their offices however they wanted, and they even got the furniture they wanted. In our minds, this was a step forward, and we were making progress and growing as a business. I think this is the mind-set that most entrepreneurs and business owners have. This was the next level. Success, right? We'd made it! Private offices— and everybody had a window. It was really nice. It forced a lot of changes because everyone needed phone extensions and things like that.

About two years later, I noticed that a lot of people were having conversations behind other people's backs. We started getting team members rallying together against their coworkers. This could have been due to other things, but I attribute it to the way the office was laid out. It allowed team members to lock themselves in their offices, have private conversations, and plan "attacks" against their co-workers, or set up exclusionary events in or out of the office.

I realized this layout wasn't the best for building a team, bringing my team together, or collaborating and sharing ideas. Every time I wanted to talk to somebody, I had to schedule a time and make sure where we were meeting. Every time that there was something minor that could have been addressed easily, it often got bigger because we couldn't react quickly enough. Because of the way the office was laid out, we had to schedule a meeting to talk about every issue. There were walls, both literally and figuratively, between everybody.

"Create a layout that's best for building a team, bringing a team together, and collaborating and sharing ideas."

When we changed offices again, we were forced to have a different layout, and we wanted to try something new based on our budget at the time available. We said, "Well, we have this big room. There's no money to put up walls, so let's just leave it open, and later we'll build private offices if we want."

In this office layout, everyone got to work in one office, in one big room. The unique thing about this was that it wasn't just the team members, but it was also the leaders and the CEO. That was different from the first layout. We made sure we weren't working back to back with each other; the team members faced each other all the time. It was amazing to see the amount of progress we made both in goal achievement and in becoming a better, stronger team. If there was a conversation that somebody was having over the phone, and he needed a quick answer, somebody else in that big room would overhear the conversation and be able to chime in. Things were addressed so quickly and efficiently. It was the same people and the same team; the only variable that was changed was the layout.

I have to confess, this wasn't done on purpose; it happened because of budget constraints. But the result was that we became so unified as a team we gained excitement about everything we did.

Obviously, there's been a lot of success and failure with open-office layouts. There's a lot of criticism about this type of layout, but from my experience, I think it unifies a team—especially millennials, who crave unification, collaboration, and a family unit in the workplace. They love this. It's also brought the rest of my team together, millennials or not. You come closer together because of the way an office is laid out. You can ask anyone on my team right now, and they'll tell you they never want to go back to the previous layouts. It is crazy and mind-blowing to me because I would never have thought that this was the way everybody would like best. But many people love working together, and they love collaborating on ideas. Ideas flow so much faster, and we can be much more efficient because we are constantly aware of what everybody's doing. We celebrate everybody's successes as they happen. We can address issues immediately because we're in the same room. It's one of those things that I think will benefit the entire company.

This is taking advantage of what I talked about earlier about experience. Millennials want an experience, and my team prefers the experience of collaboration, being in the same room, and being on the same team.

CRITICAL AREAS

Knowing what I know now, if I were to give you a checklist of what you should think about if you are setting up a new office, I would mention six critical areas. In my opinion, these contribute to the success of the way your office is laid out and the positive effect it will have on your team.

1. Common Work Space

The first critical area is the one we just talked about: a big, common workspace where everyone in the company, including the leaders, works together. Everybody's on the same playing field. Millennials want access to the top, and they want access to the right person at all times. I think that a lot of employees of other generations want the same thing as well. My employees don't want to feel like there is this glass ceiling between me and them. This glass ceiling that means that I can't reach them without going through certain steps or visa-versa. This common workspace is one of the most productive things that we've ever done in our company. The open office has increased our business success as well as personal feelings of success.

2. A Private Office for All

The second area that I think is critical is a private office. In our space, we only had room for one private office. This room is a place where we can close the door and have a private conversation. Most of the time, it's used by the manager or by the leader to have one-on-one conversations with any team member individually. It can be used for something that requires a lot of focus too—for example, meeting with a new technician to go over some basic training. We want to do this one-on-one meeting without distracting the rest of the team. This office is also used for interviewing new candidates. The private office is definitely a need. However, it's important that it's not assigned to anybody and that everybody can use it at any time, for whatever reason.

This will also prompt your team members to naturally collaborate with each other and come up with ideas, which is very important. Sometimes two people have an idea, and they want to discuss it without distracting the team, or they might want to surprise the team. They'll want a place where they can sit down, collaborate, brainstorm, and come up with good ideas, solutions to problems, and integrated ways of doing things. You want to be able to facilitate a space for these types of activities for your team.

3. A Brainstorming/Whiteboard Room

The third critical area that I want to talk about is a brainstorming room or a whiteboard room. This is important in our office—we need to have that room. I always say that this is where all the magic happens. This is where we come up with our newest ideas. Every time we want to brainstorm or set new goals, we use this room. Big companies like Google and Apple facilitate this kind of room because it gets the creative juices flowing. This room should be filled with posters of motivational things that get your team inspired and pumped up.

For some of our meetings and brainstorming, we bring out giant Post-Its. We write things on them and then paste them all over the wall. This is what this room is for. You bring your entire team, or your executive team, together to be creative, and this is the room you want to use. It's for coming up with ideas and constantly bringing up things we could do differently that we may not have thought about. It really lends itself for thinking outside the box because there are no right or wrong answers in this room; people can say anything that comes to their minds and be as creative as they want. In our office, we keep very comfortable couches as the seating in this room. We want our team to relax, be comfortable, and set the tone for everyone to be as open and creative as possible.

4. A Meeting/Goal-Tracking Room

The next room I want to talk about is a meeting room or a goal-tracking work room. It can be incorporated in a different room, but there should be a space in your office that's dedicated to having your daily, weekly, and monthly meetings. In our office, it's a space where we have a big conference/dining room table. At this table, we sit down and have every one of our meetings. All over the walls, we have plastered our KPIs for each position in our company, and we have huge charts that track everything we're doing. If you walk into this room, you can immediately understand where our company is on every single KPI and on all of our goals.

> **"We have thermometers that indicate how close we are to reaching our goals. We have all kinds of fun little things. Everybody can see our goals achievements and millennials feel like they're in the loop and have the inside scoop."**

It's a neat thing to have because everyone in the company can get a sense of how we're doing at any minute of any day. Every position is listed on huge daily trackers that have every day for the year on them. Everybody reports their particular KPIs that they're working on and they are tracked on this wall. We also have our weekly meetings in this room, so every KPI that's talked about during our weekly meetings is up on a different big poster. Everybody gets to fill and shade in. We have thermometers that indicate how close we are to reaching our goals. We have all kinds of fun little things. Our quarterly projects, our quarterly goals, and our quarterly celebrations are listed in this office. We'll change that once a quarter, and everybody can watch how we're doing.

This is important because you want everybody on your team, especially millennials, to have the inside scoop. They want to know what's going on, and they don't want to be kept in the dark on the company's progress. Part of them contributing to the team is knowing how the team is doing at all times. Big corporate America likes to put up barriers so nobody knows what others are doing. People only know about their departments, and that's it. This room is great for millennials because they get pumped up when they know what's going on. Good or bad, it doesn't matter. What matters is that they are kept in the loop, and they get excited about knowing where we are at all times.

This leads us back to two of the things I talked about earlier. The first, is making it fun—game-ifying everything that you can. Get the numbers up, along with a scoreboard that everybody is working on. The second, is having access to the top. Millennials don't want to feel like there's a hierarchy and that they're a peon without access to the leaders. They want to feel like they're responsible for the results that the company's generating. It makes total sense to have this kind of room, and it's one of the most important rooms that we have in our company right now.

5. A Break or Lunch Room

The next room I want to talk about is a simple break or lunch room. A lot of the creative conversations and innovative ideas occur in this room. You hear all the time about conversations around the water cooler—this is where they happen. People on your team want to have lunch together, and they want to exchange dialogue about what's going on in their day. Millennials always try to incorporate their life with their work. In this room, you want to create an atmosphere where everybody can have lunch or take a break together, have a snack, or talk about what they're eating and how healthy their diet is. This room should be separated from the work area, so they can sit down and relax without having to leave the office to have a personal connection with their coworkers.

6. A Culture Room

The last critical room, if your budget allows it, is what I call the culture room. This is the room you can dedicate to something that's really important and is tailored to your company's culture. If everybody's into fitness, being in shape, exercising, and eating healthy, then you want a room that's dedicated to that. Maybe everybody at your company is more on the artsy side. Have a room where people can come and do art.

Find out what drives your team and make a room that's dedicated to that. Maybe you have a team of computer programmers, and they're all into gaming. Facilitate a room for that. Maybe you have a team that has a lot of moms, and they all have young kids. What happens in that case? You have to understand that there's going to be plenty of teacher workdays or days when school kids are sick and some of these moms are not going to be able to have a place to take them. Why not create a room that facilitates bringing their kids to work? Kids can enjoy it and have fun. Maybe they can have a Wii™ or a PlayStation®. Have certain areas for the younger ages with coloring books so they can have fun at the office. You want to communicate that your culture welcomes moms to bring their kids to work, that it's not a nuisance, and that there's space for them.

In our company, we've created a music room because everybody is a music fanatic. We have a room with a big computer where anybody can sit and produce music. We have all the latest software, so anyone can actually make beats and compose their own music. We have some pianos that they can play and a very nice speaker system, so people can really enjoy the music. Anytime we have a celebration, we use the sound system in there because music is such a big part of our lives. This music room is critical for us.

"This is our culture. This is what we're all about. You're welcome to come into this room, into these spaces, and take advantage of these things, because this is what we believe and live by."

This room lets your team feel like they're really breathing their culture. They will talk about it with all of their friends. They'll tell every single person they know how cool this room is, how cool the office is, because it's 100 percent catered to what the company is all about. It's tailored to what the culture is all about. When their friends are stuck at big corporate America, and they have nothing even remotely similar to this, you're going to attract much more valuable talent because you have your office laid out in a way that's staying true to your culture. You're not just talking the talk—you're now walking the walk. "This is our culture. This is what we're all about. You're welcome to come into this room, into these spaces, and take advantage of these things, because this is what we believe and live by."

Remember, millennials intertwine their work and their personal lives; they want to mesh it all together. Providing a break or lunch room where your team can get together, a culture room, a room for meetings and tracking goals, another room for brainstorming, and an area where everybody's working together but has the possibility of a private office—this is what they really look for. At the end of the day, I think everybody on your team will benefit from it, and everybody's going to enjoy this type of atmosphere. In my experience in different office layouts, this layout was the best by far and gave us the greatest success.

In the end, each company is going to have its own solution when it comes to the office layout. It should be the physical and visual manifestation of its culture. A lot of big companies have these vision or mission statements, but they never incorporate them into real life. Nobody knows or cares about them. When I talk about creating the culture, it needs to be 100 percent alive and evident in your office. It needs to be so thick in the air that anybody who walks in there will either resonate with it or be completely turned off by it. It comes with the layout, the décor, the team—it comes with everything. You need to be adamant about bringing the culture to life in your company. Again, that comes from the leader, who puts those things in place so the team knows that you're walking the walk. "This is our culture, this is what we're all about, and it's not going away. These are our core values, this is what we believe in, and it's going to be here to stay from now until the end of time."

It works as an amazing recruitment filter as well. As we bring in candidates for face-to-face interviews, the right person will be extremely excited by all this, and the wrong person will be completely turned off by it and will most likely disappear after the interview. That's fine, and that's what we want. This is a preview into what they're getting. This is what it's going to be like, and when they walk through the doors, we're going to know that these people are the real deal.

Lastly, these six critical areas remind me of some of the most professionally designed spaces we come in contact with. Consider the way common areas at colleges are built today, and the way hotel lobbies are designed. You notice a trend to create this open, flowing environment where people can work. When they need a moment to themselves, they can easily find a private spot away from everybody and then get right back to the main area when it's time to interact again. Clearly, it's in a place like this where people want to spend their time.

CHAPTER 4 RECAP: OFFICE LAYOUT

- Create a layout that encourages team building and idea sharing.
- Open office layouts— with management included— can increase enthusiasm, idea creation, and problem solving as it unifies your team.
- Offer one private office any team member or members can use when they need focus or private conversations.
- Create a brainstorming/whiteboard room with places to share ideas, innovate, motivate, and get the juices flowing.
- Dedicate space for a meeting or goal-tracking room. Let everyone see your tracking and achievements. Make it fun. Game-ify it.
- A break or Lunch room offers a more relaxed place to connect with friends and share conversation and ideas.

- Create a culture room that fits with your company's values and the needs and likes of the workforce. Let your team feel like they've got a cool place.
- The office layout helps you incorporate the company culture into every part of office life.

For the most up-to-date material and additional information on millennials and to watch quick videos that dive deeper into these concepts, please visit my website: www.MeetJavierMontes.com

RETAINING PRODUCTIVE MILLENNIALS

WE'VE TALKED ABOUT how to understand millennials, what their thought process is, and how to create spaces to reflect what they want out of life and work. Now let's talk about how we retain them. There are a couple things on which we really want to focus in this chapter. How do we keep them on board and excited about what they are doing? And how do we keep them growing within the company without leaving?

I think a big issue that many companies face now is that millennials are switching jobs a lot. They're constantly looking for a different job or a different opportunity. I have been fortunate enough to have every person who works for my company stay with us long-term. I've never had one person intentionally resign a position with our company. That's huge! But how exactly did I manage to achieve that?

Personal Development, Not Higher Salaries

Honestly, I wasn't sure what made them stay! So I talked to my team and asked them, "Why don't you leave? I don't want you to leave, but what do you love about working here? What is it that's here that gets you so excited, where you want to continue to be here and be part of this team?" The stand-out answer was personal development. Every single person on my team, 95 percent of which are millennials, wants to learn more skills. People want to constantly develop the toolbox of what they already know.

Contrary to popular belief, they're not primarily interested in higher salaries. A lot of times, managers think they need to consistently increase their salaries and give them more money in order to maintain and retain employees. That's not necessarily the case. Often I've recruited people to come work for me for less than they are currently making because they are excited about the opportunity. They understand that I'm going to invest in developing them. I care about them— helping them and teaching them new skills. This is one of the most important things millennials look for when deciding whether to work for a company. "Does the leadership team really care about my personal development, or are they just interested in having me produce for them?"

Millennials are extremely passionate about learning. They want to expand their horizons when it comes to their abilities. We leaders need to be true to that and care about it. I think there's been a big roadblock for many entrepreneurs and managers at big companies. They come up against the mentality that says, "I need to hold them down. I can't teach them because they'll take my job." It's one of the things that drives me crazy.

"In my company, you cannot get a promotion unless you have trained somebody to do your job 100 percent. If you want to get promoted, then you need to develop somebody under you."

In my company, you cannot get a promotion unless you have trained somebody to do your job 100 percent. Every single person on my team knows that. If you want to grow within our company, if you want to move on and get promoted, then you need to develop somebody under you. You need to coach others and teach them to do everything that you know how to do. If you don't do that, you will never move up. Basically, you only hold yourself back if you withhold information from the people below you.

This gives me two things. When a person is ready to take on more responsibilities and grow within the company, he's already trained somebody as a replacement for his job. Also, he has the understanding that we are a team. You are not here by yourself, and you're not going to climb this ladder without your team. Until you learn to pull others up and teach them what you know and do, you will not move up in our company. It's part of our culture. Our culture is that we work as a team, as a family. I lead by teaching everything I know to every single team member. If they are willing to listen, I'm willing to teach them. If they're willing to learn, I'm willing to coach them through it. I'm not going to do it for them, and I'm not going to necessarily push information or knowledge down their throats.

This is what Millennials want and need. They've have a hard time finding this in today's workplace— especially in corporate America— because people are so fearful of losing their jobs to the lower salaried, younger generation. It blows my mind that leadership is creating this type of culture and constantly feeding it. We have the responsibility as leaders to change this idea. That culture is a recipe for failure. You must promote and develop people in order to grow as a society.

HIRE EXPECTING TO TRAIN

I expect to train. I hire based on mind-set, not skill set. People who come to work for our company don't necessarily know how to do the things that I hired them to do. I teach them and train them. My team will train and develop them. They will learn how to get the skill set that I need because they have the right mind-set. If you've got the right mind-set and the right ideas, and if you live and breathe our values, then the skill set part is very simple. My entire sales team is full of people who had never sold anything in their entire lives before they came to our company. You'd say that's crazy. Who would hire people for a sales position who had no sales experience? These millennials wanted to learn how to sell, but they didn't know how to do it. Part of the face-to-face interview process is a test of their sales skills. Every single one of them did pretty badly. Today, they are doing amazing things at our company because they have the right mind-set, and we were willing to teach them how to get the job done. One inherent advantage to this kind of hiring is that they didn't come with any bad habits, so they can learn how to do things our way. It makes things much easier when someone comes into a role without having predetermined ways to complete their tasks and responsibilities. Still, most business owners and big companies are very hesitant to invest the time and the effort to develop people with no experience or skill set.

"When you hire for mind-set, not skill set, you:

- Don't have bad habits or pre-determined ways to do a job
- Expand your talent pool
- Can pay less
- Reduce your risk of turnover"

But by hiring salespeople with no sales experience, I expanded my options. Now the talent pool is significantly bigger than it would be if I were looking for people with, say, three years of sales experience. Also, I reduced the risk of them expecting a lot of money, because they're not that experienced. There is always a big risk when bringing on a new employee. There is always the possibility of the person leaving or underperforming and you have to start the whole hiring process over again. What we're doing is putting people right into the fire, teaching and coaching them along the way.

For me and my business, it's the only way that works. I didn't set out to hire somebody with no sales experience. It just worked out that way; but these people were the perfect candidates for our culture. Yes, if they had had more experience, that would have been great, but my screening wasn't based on them having sales experience. I simply wanted to know how much sales ability they had. Millennials want personal development so they are easy to train. Development is not a one-time thing. I taught my sales team how to sell and will continue to develop them into better sales people until the end of time.

How can I keep developing them further? Every year when I sit down with our team for reviews, we talk about their personal goals, what they want to earn, and what they want to do. If our team can't help them learn these things— if we don't have the tools in place or if we don't have the experience to teach them— we have a different conversation about possibly not moving forward together. It's not necessarily about their performance; it's about what the company can do for them as well. This is a big part of our company culture. This is part of the life here at EMG. We are serious about this. So many people are fearful of teaching team members new skills because they feel they're going to leave them. I don't really worry about that. Ironically, it's turned out to be one of the top reasons why my team stays with me.

Something I have learned though my life is that so much of our fear is unfounded. And not only is it unfounded, but things actually turn out to be the opposite of what we thought. You fear training your team members and having them leave after they become more valuable. The reality is that one of the biggest and strongest retention builders is teaching and learning. You get far more loyal employees because they'll be afraid to take that next, better-paying job. They'll wonder, "Am I going to get the same support? Am I going to be as successful at the next job? Here they're doing everything they can to make me successful." That's what will keep your people around— especially millennials. We're talking about personal development, not higher salaries.

This reminds me of an interesting post on social media that I saw the other day:

> CFO asks CEO: What happens if we spend money training our people and then they leave?

> CEO: What happens if we don't and they stay?

Here's a critical point. Often the business owner of a smaller company or a manager at a larger company is a baby boomer or Gen Xer who is motivated by money, company car, or a bigger office. Remember, your employee may not be motivated by those things. When you are doing the review and getting feedback to figure out how to incentivize the worker, realize that it's not about what you want or what motivates you. It's about what the person on the other side of the table wants. This difference in wants and motivations sometimes makes teaching and coaching so difficult to do as well.

This is part of the reason why I wrote this book. I want to give Gen Xers and baby boomers an insight into how millennials think and what they want. I want to help today's leaders learn about millennials and recognize their traits are not good or bad, just different.

STRUCTURE, NOT MICROMANAGING

In addition to personal development, millennials are searching for structure. They want to take risks, but they also want stability. As they are trying to learn new things, they want to know that they're going to be a part of a system that works. They want the structure of a big organization, but they want the culture of a start-up. It's our job as leaders to give them that structure so they can put the pieces together and run with it. Down the line, they may even figure out a way they can do a certain process faster and smoother than you could have imagined. The key is to avoid micromanagement. We need to teach them the whole process, not breath over their shoulder and make sure they do it just the way we would. But also, we should not merely turn them loose and say "good luck."

We want to give them the structure and tell them how you do it. If we're going to teach sales, tell them how to make a sale. You start by making your first phone call. Then you put it into your CRM and schedule a follow-up task. Then you send an email, and so on. This is the structure to follow. You don't tell them, "Hey, just go make a sale." They're not going to know what to do with that. That process is too far down the line for them to really visualize it.

"Structure comes with expectations. This is how we lead them, as opposed to managing them. It's our job as leaders to make these expectations as understandable as possible."

We also want to give them expectations. The structure comes with expectations. This is how we lead them, as opposed to managing them: "We are expecting you to do this because it leads to success. This is what we do. This is how successful people on our team have done it. These are the expectations for every week and every month." We need to be very clear about expectations and it's our job as leaders to make them as understandable as possible. We need to spend time creating this structure; this helps the entire wheel come full circle. Expectations and structure are based on KPIs and how we measure them. If we give unlimited time off, they must know the KPIs they have to meet. This frees me to quit monitoring their time because it's not important; I care about their output. Their output is measured by the expectations we set for them. When the time comes to review them and rate their performance, it's a very objective conversation.

With previous generations, things were typically subjective. That's not the way that they need to be with millennials. "This is the structure, these are the expectations, and this is what I need you to do. When we have a review, we check whether or not you did it." It's a yes or a no.

In my company, we use a scorecard for every single position, and everybody is held accountable. We decide together what the expectations are. We put them in the scorecard because every new hire needs to be able to yield a certain amount of output. I don't bend expectations for different people based on their strengths or weaknesses. I expect them to learn and shoot for it, and to get up to speed with what we need them to do. From there, their natural ambition and drive will blow away those expectations. That's my experience. Everybody on my team has done that. Their innate nature is to exceed all of the expectations.

"The innate nature of millennials is to exceed all of the expectations."

The expectations are set as minimums. They give me a very objective way to be able to decide, especially with a new hire, whether or not this person is going to be successful in our organization. We've gotten so good that we've been able to identify somebody not meeting expectations within their first week. I have had a new member start with us on Monday, and by Wednesday I was letting them go. It's that clear and objective. I know day by day during their first two weeks whether they're going to be able to cut it and fit into our culture. I think that's part of the goal. Every business owner should be able to have that type of clarity for every position in the company. I think the number one reason why businesses fail, especially small businesses, is that they're too quick to hire and too slow to fire. We spend too much time, effort, and resources on a bad hire—I believe a bad hire can cost a company somewhere between three and ten times the person's salary. That's a lot of money and a very expensive mistake.

"The number one reason why businesses fail, especially small businesses, is that they're too quick to hire and too slow to fire."

That's why I'm willing to take a risk on somebody who doesn't have any sales experience. My expectations are so clear that within the first week, I can see where my investment is. If I was paying you a $50,000 salary, an investment for a week to know that you're not going to make it is not $50,000. It's much, much less than that. Am I willing to make that investment to possibly have a rock star? Yes, I'll do it every time because I can know day-by-day whether this person is going to make it. As soon as I feel like they're not, I cut them quick. But if you don't have these clear metrics in place, companies can drag the decision to let the person go far beyond their first year, costing the company in time, training, lost productivity, and salaries.

You might read scorecard and think it's the same as a job description. It's not. Job description tells what this person's regular roles, duties, and responsibilities are going to be on a daily basis. I think that's fine and needed. In our company, we have them to identify each position, but in the end you're expected to help out the company where needed, regardless of what role you're assigned. A scorecard is completely different. A scorecard will tell that person how I'm going to rate them and what they're doing at any given point in time. This is what I expect from them on day one; this is what I expect in week one, week two, month one, quarter one; this is what I expect at the end of year one. This is what a scorecard needs to be. I think this part goes hand in hand with the job description. It needs to be shared with the potential employees before they take on the role so that they know what's expected of them. That's clear with every single new hire that we have. Before we even talk about compensation, I talk about what I expect them to do within all of these different time frames. The person will know we're basing his success on certain key metrics at these given times. We go out as far as a year and a half for some positions. From day one, we're discussing what the expectations are twelve months from today. We spend enough time so that we are all crystal clear about the expectations.

I think that's one of the things that, not only millennials but, workers of every generation appreciate. Most people take a job and they don't really know what is expected of them. Say you take a front desk position— what does that actually mean? Are you just supposed to answer phones? If the expectation is clear and you put on it on the scorecard, it might say something like, "Needs to be able to answer the phone within two rings." I see more and more companies and entrepreneurs that don't make clear these expectations. In fact, even the owners have not thought about what they expect. It's probably in the entrepreneur's mind, but if nothing is verbalized or documented, how can your team know what your expectations are? We have to extrapolate that information, write it down, give it to our team, and be very clear about it, or else they don't know what they're supposed to give to us. They don't know what hitting the bull's-eye looks like. They can't define success. Maybe they have an idea, but it might be very different from the one you have as the leader.

Millennials ramp up this need for specifics and clarity. They're really big on understanding those expectations and on structure. For project deadlines, be specific about it. Tell them what you expect and set the actual date. "It's going to be June 30. We'll sit down at ten thirty in the morning to review it. This is the deadline."

> **"When you create the structure, you create a rhythm for the company, for millennials. We don't interrupt the daily flow with an issue that comes up, because we have a defined structure of meetings to handle it."**

Meeting times help create structure. Our company has a daily huddle every single day. It is a nonnegotiable meeting that all team members must participate in. It doesn't have to be in person; you can call in if you're not in the office. Every week we have a weekly meeting, and presence is mandatory for this one. Every month we have a monthly meeting. Every quarter we have a quarterly meeting. This is how you create structure. This is what millennials want. They want to see this structure. It can't be something you just throw out there, like, "We're having a meeting next week. Make sure you're there." When you create the structure, you create a rhythm for the company, for millennials. They know that there are certain things that are talked about, and they know what the agenda is. If I have a particular issue, there is a meeting to bring it up and possibly solve it. My team knows that depending on the type of issue or the type of situation you want to address, there is a meeting where it can be done, and they need to wait until that meeting to talk about it. We don't interrupt the daily flow, because we have a defined structure.

GIVE THEM PURPOSE

Millennials really want to have a sense of purpose. It's our job as leaders to make sure that we give them a clear sense of what their purpose is. Sometimes we can identify what our company's purpose is, and other times we're not very good at articulating it. It helps to start off by identifying what our company's purpose is and what we want to accomplish in the world. We talked a little about this in earlier chapters regarding why the company exists, what we want to accomplish, and what difference we want to make in the world as a company.

Our job as the leaders of the business is to make sure that this purpose is clear to the entire team and anybody looking to join. Once millennials join your team, they want to know exactly how their functions, tasks, and daily activities will contribute to that purpose. Therefore, you should find a way to give them their own sense of purpose in your company. It's critical for them to feel like they have a purpose, a role, and they're contributing to the overall reason the company exists. Millennials can really align themselves to your organization's purpose if it's in line with their personal purpose.

A company that lacks clear purpose will leave millennials hungry and unfulfilled. Eventually they will look elsewhere to fill that empty place.

COMMUNICATION: THE INSIDE SCOOP

In addition to the scoreboards and reporting back to them on how they're doing, I'd like to mention some of my guidelines for communicating effectively with millennials, especially if you're not part of this generation.

You've learned that millennials like a lot of praise. Remember this generation got a trophy just for showing up. They like to get frequent feedback to know how they're doing and how to improve. Another element of critical importance for the retention of millennials is their desire to get what I call "the inside scoop." What does that mean? They hate the glass ceiling where upper management is very clearly divided from the rest of the team. That leaves employees wondering what the upper management is doing, what they're planning and plotting, and whether the lower employees are included in these plots.

Millennials want to know everything—and I mean everything. In our company, we are extremely transparent when it comes to the inside scoop. Every millennial who works at our company, and every team member, knows exactly what our financials look like. They don't really care to learn how to read them in full detail, but they do care to understand whether we're doing good or bad, and what we need to do to improve. A lot of small business owners and entrepreneurs are wary about this, and you can often hear them say things like, "Oh, I don't know whether I should share my financials."

I don't share every single line item on my financials; I don't break it down for them into finite details. One of the things that is pretty taboo is talking about is how much each person is getting paid. It doesn't need to be that detailed. It needs to be more generic, answering questions like, "What do our revenues look like? What did they look like last month? What did they look like this month, last year? What are they going to look like next month? What does our cost of goods sold look like? What does our gross profit look like? What do our overhead expenses look like?" This information is invaluable to millennials.

Not only are you teaching them certain business skills, but you're teaching them the entrepreneurial mind-set because they're learning about how a business runs and makes money. At the same time, they feel like they're part of the upper management. There's no division in my company, and there shouldn't be a division in most companies, especially with millennials. They should be involved in the information that's being transmitted within the company.

This is what I mean by the inside scoop. We've also incorporated in our company what we call an executive team. In the executive team, we talk about things such as growth metrics, what are we going to do, and what new things we need to implement in order to do better and bigger things than we did last year. Everybody on my executive team is a millennial. They enjoy being part of this team because they're actively contributing to the growth of the organization on a firsthand basis.

You'll find more success with millennials when you erase the glass ceiling and start sharing with your team. Bring them on your side so they can understand. Believe it or not, they will also empathize with you when the company's struggling. When things aren't going well, they will be the first ones to volunteer and say, "What do we need to do so we can get more cash? What do we need to do so we can have more reserves?" They will be actively involved because they'll feel like they're part of the team. They'll feel like they're being included as opposed to being excluded. A good friend and successful entrepreneur Govindh Jayaraman, said when business owners struggle with a challenge in their business, they are afraid to bring the topic up to their team. They worry that their team might lose faith in the stability of the company and want to jump ship. However, Jayaraman made a strong case when he said, "If you don't bring your team up to speed on an issue that you are facing with the business, then who is going to help you get out of that issue? It is very unlikely that you will be able to solve [it] yourself, without the help and support of your team." In *Paper Napkin Wisdom* by Govindh Jayaraman & Jack Daly, you can find many more pearls of wisdom from some of the greatest entrepreneurs and thinkers. You will thank me later for that book!

"If you don't bring your team up to speed on an issue that you are facing with the business, then who is going to help you get out of that issue? It is very unlikely that you will be able to solve [it] yourself, without the help and support from your team."

Also, it's important to share changes in your team. You need to communicate why new people have come, why we have parted ways with others—whether it's their own choice or you made the change, and why the company's making decisions about growing or not growing. These are the things that millennials really have a hunger to understand, because they don't want to show up every day at the company when they don't know which way their captain is steering the ship.

When we're going to open a new position or bring on a new person, my whole team is aware of every step of the process. If we have to let go of somebody, the entire team is aware right away after it happens. This way the whole team feels like they are part of the inside scoop. They feel very comfortable because they're not going to get hit with any surprises tomorrow, and nobody's plotting against them. They feel just like when they were growing up, when they had their helicopter parents who were hovering over them and protecting them. They think, "Okay, I'm protected because I'm a part of this team. I know what I'm doing, and I know in what direction we're going."

TEACH THEM TO LEAD

I've talked about leading versus managing. Millennials, with their thirst for learning, can easily develop into leaders. One of the things we do in our company that's very successful is to give everybody on the team an opportunity to spearhead projects and new ideas. There are a lot of opportunities to lead, such as new projects or new ideas that you may want to implement, and you can start them small. Every person needs to be in charge of something.

I'm not asking you to tell them to lead the whole company, or to lead an entire department. What I'm saying is that there are projects and plenty of opportunities in every company, where you can allow somebody to shine and spread his/her wings, to be a leader and see what it feel like, and to understand the ownership and the responsibility that comes along with it. The true leaders will rise from the woodwork, and before you know it, you have an entire team full of leaders. This is ultimately what you want.

In many companies, when there's a new project to lead or spearhead, you go to the middle or upper management of the company. Somebody on the lower level has no chance to lead until they have worked up to a position of manager. I constantly get approached by managers and business owners who complain that millennials don't stay at a job long— maybe a year or less before they move on. My first question to them is, "Are you giving the millennials an opportunity to lead? Have you given them any projects where they feel like they are responsible and have the ability to exercise this part of their brains to be leaders? Or are you constantly holding them down and clipping their wings? Are you indirectly telling them that they need to stay down and can't come up here, because they're not part of the secret team?" Typically they look surprised. Of course they haven't.

It doesn't have to be anything with outward exposure; it could be internal. Sometimes we do it with planning a birthday party for one of the employees. We let one of the new millennials do it, and we see how it goes. This gives them an opportunity to lead, and also, it gives us leaders the chance to coach them, guide them, and say, "Hey, let's do this, and let's set a goal. Let's brainstorm and see who's going to be responsible for what, and let's assign tasks to certain people." That's what a leader is. Luckily, my entire company is made up of leaders—not because they came on board as leaders, but because I've given them the opportunity to try to lead, and wherever they fell short, we coached and helped them so that they've developed into leaders. At the end of the day, that's what all of us want for our companies. We want a company full of leaders, but we're hesitant to train them because we're afraid that they will leave us within a short time.

It takes a lot of courage to take somebody who's in an entry level position and new in your company, and to put them in charge of something.

However, this is the greatest and fastest way to develop leadership traits among your team. All of these things are going to require some work, so why not take your team and put them in charge so they can have a fair chance at demonstrating their leadership abilities?

CREATE BONDING OPPORTUNITIES

Earlier I mentioned the need for employees to bond. Now let's look deeper into this concept and how to do this correctly.

As we try to maintain our team and retain them for the long run, one of the things we've gotten very good at is creating opportunities for bonding during work and work activities. It's imperative for your entire team to find things that they have in common. This is how we all develop relationships. We talked about how millennials intertwine their personal and business lives. If this is true, then it makes sense we should give them the chance to get to know each other better. We've identified that they are a good culture fit and proceeded to bring them on to the team, but the team doesn't know them yet. In fact, you don't know them that well either.

How do you get to know somebody? Well, just doing your work and just going through your normal activities won't lend itself to getting to know a person on a nonprofessional level. In our company, I found it helpful to purposely create activities that connect our team on a personal level. This happens most easily by holding events during business hours when they're still in their business mind-set. We do things that allow them to expand and share their personal interests in hopes that they will quickly find common ground with others on the team, so they can develop deep friendships with their coworkers.

Organizing and executing these activities is definitely not the easiest task, but I assure you that it will have one of the highest ROI for your team. Its important to not get too lost in the details of the activities because there are simple traditional things you can do too— like happy hours. In our company, we are known for thinking outside the box and often coordinating team outings. These are strictly things that are team-building activities, fun activities, things that the team can enjoy together. These are a little bit difficult to do so we challenge ourselves to be creative. As I mentioned, 90 percent of millennials want their team members to be their friends too. I found that purposely creating opportunities for the team to bond and find commonalities develops a much stronger bond. By doing this, your team members are less likely to leave to go work for somebody else or look for other opportunities, because they feel like they're part of a family and have their friends here. They have a sense of responsibility to the rest of the team because they've gotten to know each other. They've developed close friendships with their coworkers. Why would somebody want to go work for another company where they don't know whether they'll get along with those people, and they're already happy here? This approach develops long-term retention with millennials.

If you hear Tony Hsieh talk about what he thinks makes Zappos so successful, he will tell you it's that their entire business plan is developed around creating a friendship environment. They actually hold people accountable to make sure that they're developing relationships with the people they manage. By doing so, they improve their performance and overall satisfaction at the workplace.

CHAPTER 5 RECAP: RETAINING PRODUCTIVE MILLENNIALS

- Millennials are more attracted by personal development opportunities than by larger salaries.
- Create a culture where promotions come only after they've thoroughly trained people below them to do their job.
- Set the standard by leaders teaching team members all they are willing to learn.

- Hire based on mind-set, not skill-set and then teach them how to do the job.
- Personal development isn't a one time teaching, it's ongoing.
- Give millennials the process and the structure to follow. Don't micromanage and don't just turn them loose without proper training.
- Expectations allow you to lead without seeming to "manage" them. KPIs help you establish and monitor the expectations you set.
- Share financials, problems, and changes with millennials so they know the inside scoop.
- Provide leadership opportunities and bonding opportunities to keep millennials happy at your company

For additional details on the characteristics of millennials and to watch quick videos that dive deeper into each of these, please visit my website: www.MeetJavierMontes.com

CHAPTER 6

LEADING MILLENNIALS

ONCE YOU HAVE millennials on your team and incorporated into your culture, it's imperative you understand how to manage them. In Chapter 2 we discussed that millennials want to be led, not managed. In this chapter, I'll cover some of the most effective practices I've used and that are simple enough to implement almost immediately into your organization.

SHORT-TERM DEADLINES

I use the word manage loosely because I don't want you to actually manage somebody in the traditional method that we associate with the word manage. Let's define the word manage to cover how to organize, lead, and empower your team at the same time you make sure that they're contributing to the success of the organization and the goals we want to achieve. The first best practice is implementing short-term deadlines. Pre-millennial generations come from a different time period, where they're always talking about planning for the future, and their future is usually a year or longer out. Millennials don't think ahead for more than two or three months. Planning a project, a deadline, or a goal that's further out than three months is almost unfathomable for them. If we know that, then we shouldn't plan or instigate projects that will not let them visualize the end result, because it's too far away for them to fully grasp the expected outcome and/or develop a plan to accomplish it.

I am not suggesting that you omit any long-term planning from your organization. You still need to set up your one- and three-year goals, your BHAG (Big Hairy Audacious Goal), and set up what you want to accomplish before the end of the year. However, you typically do these once a year and have them posted visibly at your office so your entire team can be constantly reminded of these targets throughout the year. What I am suggesting is that you want to break down these targets into quarterly steps of how you're going to get there. If possible, break it down into 3-4 week chunks. This is the ideal time horizon in which millennials live their lives. This is what their mind can clearly articulate. This is what they'll feel excited about and feel in control to realistically complete. For projects or tasks that will last more than 3 months, I have found that millennials tend to struggle much more. They get disillusioned and frustrated within the first few weeks and rarely are able to see these tasks through to completion.

Quarterly goals are amazing, for example. They are amazing short-term goals and one of the most powerful elements we have in our company today. Naturally, they are also one of the things that almost always get accomplished at EMG. Why? We found it's because it's so relevant for our millennial team. Millennials can address these targets almost instinctively. Every time we create new projects and new products, 99 percent of the time, they are for the upcoming quarter. Everything at EMG has to end in a quarter. Even if I know something's going to take me two quarters, or even three or four quarters, I look at that and say, "What can I accomplish by the end of this quarter?" That's what we focus on, and that's how we achieve the results. Anything outside of that, we tend lose focus on, and we end up not accomplishing it because it's just so far away for millennials to visualize and fully own.

The truth is, millennials want to see instant results. Break it up into bite-size pieces for them, into fully digestible goals, measurements, accomplishments, and projects, because then they see from the beginning to end what it looks like. If you want to lead your team properly, you need to set them up in a position to win from the beginning. Focus on that. Keep all your timelines on short-terms, and keep them moving. That's the name of this game. As your team continues to push the ball forward, focus on what's happening in the next couple of weeks, or in the next month or so, and quickly watch your millennials become some of the most valuable members on your team.

It's very important that you clearly set your deliverables and expectations. Have your team come up with them and give them to you. Present them so everyone knows exactly what you expect the next week. If you help them easily define success for next week, they will be able to visualize it, execute on it, and find the instant gratification that they crave. This propels them into massive action for the following week. Each weekly success takes you one step closer to your one-year goal. I say this about millennials specifically, but the reality is that everybody in the workforce will get fired up by using this system, because you are lining up a set of quick wins to celebrate their progress; and everybody likes to be a winner!

> **"Millennials want to see instant results. We train our new employees in a way that lets them take actionable items and see results right away."**

This system also changes the way we train our new employees. We set them up with actionable items that let them see results right away. During training with previous generations, we taught them about planning and patiently waiting for results; you learned habits, tools, and shortcuts that would give you results—over time. Six months or a year down the line, if you're consistent with the actions you do, you might be up to speed. The millennial generation wants to see the results now. In order to accomplish that, we have to bite-size the training and give them tools, tips, and tricks that they can implement today, and which they'll start seeing results in the next few days or weeks. The advantage with all generations is they retain the learning best when they apply it immediately.

Without this method of training, it is quite common to see millennials lose excitement about a new position. If we don't train them in a way that lets them take action and see results right away, a high turnover should be expected.

I'll finish off this concept by adding that generations before the millennials couldn't google answers to questions they faced. For them, it was critical to learn every possible answer to every possible question during training for a new position. In today's fast moving and ever-so-changing world, it seems that it is almost impossible to keep our team "fully" trained at all times. However, with today's technology it's not necessary at all to train on all scenarios; it's just important to train our team on how to find the answers, whenever they might need them.

Remember when we were kids in school and we asked, "Why do I need to learn all these multiplication tables? I'm always going to have a calculator." The teacher said, "You may not have a calculator in front of you one day." Now we look back and laugh, because all of us have a calculator in our pockets, on our phones. We have no reason to have a phone book anymore. Information is so much more available that I think it changes what we should be asking these people to master and learn. We can say, "We've got all this documented. There's a knowledge base here, and it's always going to be here when you need it, so don't worry about it." It's similar to the "just in time" learning. I find that a younger workforce rejects having to memorize things that seem pointless to them, or having to learn things that they might use "one day." They're more protective of their brain space. They want to learn the fundamentals, they want to learn the reason behind things, and they want to know they can look up the how-to when they actually need it.

Finally, some people think you can't get a lot done in just thirteen weeks— a quarter. But if you don't keep your eye on the ball, you'll wake up, and it'll be over. I'm sure that you have heard the adage, "Most people overestimate what they can accomplish in a month, but grossly underestimate what they can accomplish in a year." I'm here to tell you that millennials don't suffer from that syndrome. While it's true that a millennial won't be focused on a year from now, a millennial is so focused and motivated by the immediate short term successes, that he will almost always accomplish much more than his non-millennial counterpart. It's time to start harnessing the power of this generation and capitalizing on this strong asset of millennials.

Constant Feedback

That brings me to my next point: feedback. Feedback is critical for millennials. This is one of those things that I've talked about in several sections of the book. It doesn't matter if it's good or bad—millennials want feedback. Some people say that millennials are addicted to feedback. And if you don't give them what they're addicted to, they're going to lose motivation or get distracted. I can't say this enough: give them constant feedback. For some of us, it's difficult. I know, because it is very difficult for me, too. What I found works better for me is to schedule the time to give feedback, and I plan those days ahead.

> **"Millennials are addicted to feedback. And if you don't give them what they're addicted to, they're going to lose motivation or get distracted."**

If you're bringing on a new hire, you can say, "Well, we're going to check in when you're one week into it. We're going to check in thirty days into your position. We're going to check in sixty days. This is how we're going to do it." A lot of times we say that, but we never really follow through, or thirty days becomes thirty-one or thirty-two days. It gets drowned out because there'll be other important things that need your attention. I recommend that as soon as you plan something, immediately schedule the feedback on your calendar. If you brought in a new hire and you said that you're going to give feedback during the first week, schedule it on the calendar immediately. Everyone can see this is the time and date you're going to talk about feedback. "After

JAVIER MONTES

thirty days, it's going to be April 30 at 2:00 p.m., we're going to sit down for half an hour, and I'm going to give you feedback on your progress thus far."

In order to achieve the highest level of performance from millennials, this is the proper feedback system to put into place. This can be a very daunting task for managers of previous generations. But don't be intimidated by this, because the truth is this small thing only costs us a little time on our calendar and it will give us one of the biggest returns from our millennial workforce. At the end of the day, don't you want your team to execute in a way that is effective and efficient for you? How can your team know the direction you want to go, if you're not telling them what they're doing right and what they're doing wrong along the way? If they start to veer a little bit to the right, you say, "No, no, it's time to get back to the left." If you aren't doing this on a constant basis, your team can end up being extremely far right before you catch it and exclaim, "You're way off track, and you need to get back to the left." This strategy can end up costing your organization an exorbitant amount of wasted capital and resources.

While we may feel awkward or apprehensive about offering feedback, millennials love it. Initially, I found giving feedback very challenging and daunting. I used these three steps to make it easier and more comfortable for both of us.

1. Keep it frequent. When you give feedback once a month, you don't have a large build-up to cover.
2. Keep it simple. Address just the vital issues.
3. Create a simple format to keep you on track.
4. Keep it short. Millennials are satisfied with quick feedback.

I recommend that, at a minimum, feedback happens monthly with every single millennial on your team. In fact, I would recommend it for every employee on your team, and I wouldn't wait longer than a month in between each feedback session.

When giving feedback, it's important to keep it very simple. I noticed that past mentors and coaches I've had— myself included—tend to complicate things and make them more difficult unnecessarily. We think that our businesses are different from every other business; that they're a little bit more complicated because of one thing or another. The truth is it's not that complicated. It's just we leaders tend to make it complicated. In our company, we took about an hour to develop a simple format for executing a proper feedback session, and now these sessions are easy simple, and our entire team is excited and looks forward to them.

We have specific items that we cover in every feedback session. I developed a very small, informal agenda of what I needed to cover when I gave somebody feedback. Always keep it related to relevant facts and focused on instant results and short-term deadlines. Also, conversations should be short. Millennials don't have enough attention span to sit there and be lectured for an hour. Make it sweet and simple, and they will be satisfied and motivated.

Lastly, I have found that the more often the feedback, the better the performance. In fact, Tony Robbins makes the very few people whom he takes on as a personal health coach email their bodyweight to him every night before they go to bed. The reason he does that is because he says he can find out how productive their day was, and he can identify when people are going off the rails over a two- or three-day trend. Most coaches wouldn't know until the next time they talk to their clients a month later. It's been a big lesson to me about the faster you pulse, the better you manage performance.

**"The more often you give feedback, the
better you manage performance."**

STRONG BUT SIMPLE KEY PERFORMANCE INDICATORS

One of the challenges a lot of entrepreneurs face is developing key performance indictors (KPIs) and deciding which KPIs should be used for each position. What is a KPI really? It compares two or more different metrics in your business to give you an indication of a particular role. Either we're comparing revenues to cost, or we compare revenues to average work. That's how we develop these KPIs.

Developing the right KPIs is a big challenge for many business owners. This is something that has to be very relevant to each business on an individual basis. We have general things which we measure all the time, like annual revenue. That's a KPI, but not a strong measurement. You want to develop strong KPIs. One of my mentors told me that the more metrics that you can incorporate into a KPI, the stronger it will be. If you could incorporate a third thing that you compare in there, the KPI is going to be much stronger, and therefore more effective.

I'll give you an example. Our KPI measures revenues with a year, so we're checking the revenues for that year. If we say, "What are our gross profits for this year?" now we're comparing revenues to the cost to goods sold plus time. That's a much stronger KPI than just revenue per year. Moving the ball a little further, you can even go as deep as four different variables. For example, I want to know how much gross profit this person brought in during the last twelve months. You're comparing one employee's production to the revenue she brought in, and to the cost to goods sold during the last twelve months. That becomes an extremely strong KPI for that one role.

I'd recommend you establish clear, strong KPI for every single role in your company has. The KPI will dictate how often it should be measured. Some KPI's should be measured monthly or weekly, while others are much more effective when measured on a daily basis. That is critical. In our company, our salespeople need to submit X amount of proposals per day. I want to know how many proposals each one of my salespeople has presented each day, because that is a leading indicator for our business. Based on that number, we know exactly what percentage of those proposals we're going to close, and that will tell us exactly how much revenue we are going to have within a certain amount of time. I want to know this every single day. If somebody's numbers are not up to par, I want to catch that as early as possible. I want to have the visibility to pick up on any downward trends immediately. Therefore, we include this KPI every single day in our daily huddle. Each member of our sales team will report the number of proposals that they've turned in for that day.

I suggest you set individual KPIs for shorter times—to be measured daily, weekly, monthly, and maybe even quarterly, but I wouldn't go any farther than quarterly. Company level KPIs are usually recommended to be measured with a monthly, quarterly or yearly time frame if you want to have a strong pulse on where your company is and what direction you are headed.

At the same time, KPI's can throw up a red flag go up if somebody having a bad day or a bad week. Nine out of ten times, there's usually something going on in someone's personal life that's affecting their performance at work. A good leader should have the power to immediately identify this problem. They can then take action with that member on their team to find out what is going on, empathize with the person, and see if there is anything that the leader can do to help. You may not be able to see a life problem simply by the expressions on their faces, but it will definitely show in their work. You can sit down and have conversations with them, get feedback, and ask them, "What's going on? I noticed your numbers are down this week. For the last three days, your numbers have been down. Is there something else outside of here that's affecting you?" That sort of conversation alone will develop a strong relationship with your millennial, and you'll be developing a team for life. Sometimes just the act of asking if everything is ok goes a very long way with your team. Other times, your team member can really benefit by having the leader telling them that it's ok to take a few days off to address whatever is going on in their personal life. How much better of a leader can we be, simply by having such clarity and visibility into our company, our team, and every individual in our organization with one or two simple metrics?

PRAISE, PRAISE, PRAISE

Not only do we need to give feedback and talk about the numbers, but when millennials do things well, we need to go out of our way to recognize them. Praise is the name of the game. When it comes to millennials, we're talking about a generation where everybody got a trophy, everybody got praised, and everybody got rewarded just for showing up. When your team does something very good, you want to make sure that you praise them every opportunity you get. You have to recognize even things that seem small. This is another very challenging subject for me personally, because I'm not one to naturally give out praise. It's very difficult for me to do. I was challenged when it came to starting to work with millennials who were craving to be praised.

We did a couple of different things to make it a bit easier for me. One of the things was to set up a system where peers can give each other praise. We set up a peer-to-peer system where team members could recognize their successes among themselves when they did something well.

This was huge because it snowballed once it gained momentum amongst our team. After that, the recognition didn't stop. All of a sudden, everybody's getting praised in our weekly and daily meetings. It felt like we had this big praise festival going on in our company, and everybody's happy. The person giving the praise is happy. The person receiving the praise is happy. We've developing this very contagious positive energy in the room.

That got me involved in becoming a better manager who could give praise more easily and frequently. I learned different ways to give recognition. My Gen X training said that praise had to be given for big achievements and for big projects. I learned that I could give praise for smaller things, as well as for milestones. Why not? We don't have to wait until the end of the project to celebrate, do we? That was one of the lessons that I had to learn from my team.

"Give praise for milestones and small things. You don't have to wait until the project is finished."

Currently, we use a service called TINYpulse® (TINYpulse.com). They have a product called Cheer for Peers. It's an Internet-based system where team members can go online and recognize each other. All of our team members are listed on the website, and they can click each other and give each other praise. We use the system to integrate core values and bring them to the forefront. We said, "Feel free to recognize each other, but it needs to be tied to one of our core values. How has the person you are recognizing demonstrated one of our core values?" It's not just praising people on how they look, for example. It was now a challenge for them to keep their eyes and ears open for our core values throughout the workday, and then look for people who are exemplifying them.

Before we had that service, we used the same method, but in a handwritten physical form. At our office, we had a small box and index cards next to it, and people could submit them before the meetings or throughout the week. It's that simple. You don't need to get into anything too high-tech or complicated. You could do something in a little box that you keep in the office, and anybody can drop in anything at any time during the week. Then once a week, you can go through them. If your company's a little bit bigger, and you're getting too many, maybe you want to incorporate them in the daily huddles and get cheers for each other every time you have the daily huddle. That's the way our system works. Basically, that's peer-to-peer recognition.

The next type of recognition needed is your manager's recognition. It's one thing to be recognized by your peers, but it's another thing to get praise and recognition from a supervisor or manager. When you are getting that type of praise, you can receive it privately or publicly. Receiving the praise privately is very nice, and these are very important meetings because they're in a one-on-one atmosphere, talking with your supervisor about how good you did; it feels good. At the same time, a public type of praise from your manager in front of the whole team has much more impact. Incorporating both of these is a very good formula for success.

When we're giving praise, some of the things that I found is that we want to focus on people's strengths, not their weaknesses. Millennials feel very strongly about their strengths, so it's important to accentuate them. Focus on what they're doing really well. Don't focus so much on the fact that they're improving a particular weakness. Unless it's something that they've identified that they want to personally accomplish to get better at, I wouldn't say anything about their weakness. Millennials know what they're really good at. If you're focusing on these things, they will feel like you have aligned with them, that you're connecting with them, and that you understand who they are. Understanding your team, and having your team feel like you understand them, is one of the most powerful things you can have in any organization.

Chip Conley, author of *Peak*, says that he has a map of everybody in every organization that works for him—thousands of employees. He identifies what motivates anyone he comes in contact with or who reports to him. Are they motivated by praise, challenge, promotion, or money? Then he goes out of his way to see that that even the most underappreciated worker is praised. He wasn't specifically talking about millennials, but it's something all leaders can learn.

When we're talking about strengths and values, our strengths are often aligned to the personal values that we hold. If you're implementing my system and hiring based on culture fit, your team will have the same values as you. Focusing on their strengths should be a very easy task because their strengths are aligned with your company values. Simply identify and look for those things. It's easy to recognize and praise your team when they're doing things that they're naturally good at.

Bring Their Personal Lives to Work

Earlier, I talked about the fact that if you can create an environment of friendship, you will have amazing retention because people won't want to leave; their work lives become their personal lives as well. Of course, there are other ways to bring employees' personal lives to work so they don't feel like there's such a rigid boundary. Part of leading is to find out what's happening in your team members' lives.

When they walk through the door, they don't want to feel as if they have disconnected and entered another world. The opposite is actually true: they're bringing their personal life to work. As leaders, managers, and business owners, it's our task to acknowledge that. Then we can better know what they're going through, what they're trying to accomplish, and what goals they're there to achieve. Again, this is something very difficult for me. How do I talk with somebody about her personal life, at work? How do I get him to openly share personal things that he may not want to share or isn't comfortable speaking about? Am I probing too much? I admit, this can feel like a very difficult concept.

"During every single weekly meeting we share good news with each other. Everybody shares one personal item and one business good news that they celebrated in the last week."

One of the simple things that we do during every single weekly meeting is that we sit around the table as a team, open up, and share good news with each other. Everybody shares one personal item and one business good news that they celebrated in the last week. This is an opportunity for people to share something about their personal lives that they're happy about and are comfortable sharing with the team. Every week we get a pulse on what's going on in our entire team's lives. Recently, one of our team members got engaged, and then she started planning her wedding and hiring vendors. She's looking at a house to move into right now. She's going through things in her life that are important and memorable, and she's sharing it with her team, her second family. That's just one example. We had another employee who was remodeling her bathroom, and she was having problems with the contractor. It turns out that somebody else on the team had a contact that could help her out.

There may be things we do at the company or in the context we have that give us the opportunity to ask how things are going. Then we can understand if people on our team are a little more stressed or a little more relaxed. This is important because you're bringing them together in your company. It's part of your culture; it's part of the energy that's in your room whether you like it or not, so you might as well know what's going on and contribute to it.

You might think these things have nothing to do with your business, but it does. Work is personal for millennials; it's intertwined. This is how you get a good pulse on what's going on in your team's lives and how you connect on a more personal level than just a supervisor-employee relationship. One of the best and easiest ways to connect on a personal level is by allowing them to share the exciting things that are going on in their lives so that other team members can openly share their experiences, or help them, or join them in the rejoicing— just like they do with their families at home.

RESULTS VERSUS HOURS

Millennials are not really fans of walking in at nine and clocking out at five. One of the things that millennials value is being able to have flexible work hours. If we know that, and we're going to allow that kind of culture in our business or company, then it stands to reason that we should focus our measuring tools on results, not hours. At our company, we don't track hours; we don't really care how many hours you're working, as long as you're bringing in the results. Every single person on our team knows what they're responsible for. They are required to own that responsibility. If it takes you twenty hours a week to accomplish those results, then I'm very happy for you. If it takes you forty hours a week, then so be it. As I said, we focus on results, not hours.

We talked about this in Chapter 3. It's not so much about spending a certain amount of time sitting at your desk, answering emails, or answering phone calls. It's more about the results that you are able to contribute. At the end of the day, as a business owner, I want results. I couldn't care less if I have an employee who comes in ten minutes or half an hour before work and stays here half an hour after the office closes, if he's not being productive. That serves no purpose. I want somebody who is actively involved in accomplishing tasks. And if he can finish them quickly or get the results he wants before the deadline, then why should he have to sit at his desk for a few more hours, watching the minutes tick by until he can go home? That doesn't make sense to me.

When you set up accurate KPIs, you can be comfortable giving your employees this freedom. You've defined the rules for winning, and so you don't have to sit around and wonder whether they're getting enough done to make you profitable.

> **"The whole concept of managing millennials boils down to setting them up to win over and over again, from praise to the KPIs, the regular feedbacks, and being results-driven over hours-driven."**

The KPIs are so clear and easy for people to read on their own, that my team members always know what their results look like. They know if they're falling a bit short and need to invest more time. They also know if they've already exceeded their goals and they can choose whether they want to continue working or finish their day, go home, pick up their kids, or run errands. That's perfectly fine. In fact, that's amazing!

This whole concept of managing millennials boils down to setting them up to show them that they're winning over and over again, from praise to the KPIs, the regular feedbacks, and being results-driven over hours-driven. It sometimes feels like a video game designed specifically for my business and my team. It's great because the environment that's created through this is very electric and positive, making it a powerful way to lead and develop our workforce.

CHAPTER 6 RECAP: LEADING MILLENNIALS

- Millennials can't think years out. Break down your long-term goals into short-term deadlines of 3-4 weeks or, at most, three months.
- Train millennials in bite- sized pieces so they can take action and see results right away. Long, slow learning is a turn-off for them and results in high turn-over for your company.
- Constant feedback is essential to millennials. Schedule time to give it.
- Frequent feedback improves performance.
- KPIs, accurately measured, give you a pulse for the company and each team member.
- Use peer-to-peer recognition to keep millennials feeling praised and valued.
- Managers need to give private and public praise that focuses on the millennial's strengths.
- Connect on a personal level by asking about private as well as work successes.
- Specific KPIs let you focus on productivity instead of time in the office.

Sign up for my weekly video blog that provides some powerful insight into the millennial generation via my website: www.MeetJavierMontes.com

ATTRACTING MILLENNIALS TO JOIN YOUR TEAM

WE ALL KNOW we need more talent to grow our companies, and millennials are the greatest source of emerging talent today. It's the largest population in the United States, so chances are, we'll have millennials applying for jobs at our companies. But if we don't know how to attract millennials, we can't grow our companies. It's that simple.

> **"If we don't know how to attract millennials, we can't grow our companies. It's that simple."**

We're competing with the big companies, little companies, international companies. How are we going to stand out, attract the best of the best, and properly select the millennials who are right for our culture?

THE HIRING PROCESS

The hiring process is both a screening tool to select the right candidates and also, if done correctly, a way to attract millennials to want to join your team. I'm going to take you through my entire process, step by step. While there are quite a few steps, every step of the way is critical for attracting millennials. They make sure millennials are excited about coming on board and help them understand it is a coveted position and an exciting opportunity to join your company.

This process is a very scalable and teachable system that's easy to replicate if you have a company with several people who hire.

The Ad

The first step in the hiring process is the ad you place to get people to apply for the position at your company. Even if your company is located directly on streets filled with millennials it's unlikely you will have amazing candidates just walk in looking for a job. Really, today, few people ever walk in and ask for a job. Most job seekers visit different websites like Craigslist, Indeed, and Monster to search for career opportunities. Traditional ads from big companies tend to list everything in the form of job descriptions and responsibilities. These ads— thousands of them— quickly become overwhelming. Millennials, trying to find their place in the world, are searching for an ad that will speak to them in their language, an ad that will excite them about having fun and fulfilling their purpose in life.

They're trained in school and by their parents to seek particular jobs that work toward their strengths. But on a deeper level, they want to internally and emotionally connect with the ad. They will respond to the ones they connect with the most, and they'll also apply randomly to all the ones that they think their skill set fits well. There's something about clicking and submitting a bunch of different responses to a lot of different companies, that gives them immediate satisfaction in making progress towards getting a job. However, when they find the few ads that connect with them emotionally, they will invest a little more time in these applications.

If we know that this to be true, then this is the only way that we can effectively compete with larger organizations to attract the top talent. It's important for you to prepare your ad to connect with millennials. Your wording must help your ad stand out from the bunch. Small business owners and entrepreneurs have an advantage when competing with huge corporations who have maybe one hundred positions available at any time. It takes a little more effort to avoid the standard and generic ads. But we can compete by being very clear about what we want a person to accomplish and what an employee should expect when joining our small business, our start-up, or our growing company.

"Writing job ads to attract millennials is the only way to effectively compete with larger organizations to attract the top talent."

Let's get a bit more specific about the way to structure the ad. First, the ad needs to describe specifically what the person or the position will be helping the organization accomplish. You want to quickly describe the organization's why or purpose. "The ideal person will be able to help our company bring Internet access to every home in America." The initial inclination is to be very specific about job responsibilities and duties. However, this is not what you want to do in this ad. You want to keep this very holistic and clear. Another example could be, "We are looking for someone that is interested in helping us change the way the world celebrates." That's how we open the ad. You need be sure we connect with your why as a company. What's your purpose as a company? You need to communicate to people who are coming to work with you that this is their opportunity to help you on your course. It's vital to communicate your why message very quickly, or else the millennial may never get to it. They'll move on to the next ad.

The next part of the job ad is to state your core values. One of my mentors, Scott Fritz, showed me how simple it is to figure out what the ad needs to say. "We are a values-driven organization. Our company core values are …," then list out your core values. That's it. Make sure it's right at the top, under your why, so that whoever's reading your ad understands that these core values are extremely important at your organization. At this point in the ad, you haven't even talked about the position. State your core values, either in bullet points or a numbered list. I normally use bullet points because I don't think one is more important than the other. We mention our core values before we do anything else.

The next set of information that should be in your ad is a general description of what the position requires the person to do. This is accomplished by listing the core competencies, no less than three and no more than five, that will be nonnegotiable for this person to have. This can be worded something like: "The ideal candidates possess all of these qualities...." What's important for me is to be disciplined and to not list out everything a person will do. Again, we want to only focus on the core, nonnegotiable things that will make the right person in this position successful.

Clearly explaining what we mean is part of our challenge as entrepreneurs. Job applicants need to understand the things the applicant must have are the core competencies that you cannot train. Or perhaps it shows the candidate the weaknesses that are not compatible with the position. For example, if you're looking for somebody who's compulsively organized or extremely creative, you need the person to already have these competencies because they can't be taught. Basically, what you want to achieve with the ad is to make the ideal person—the right person—feel like he's the perfect fit for your company culture. This ad is an advertisement for the culture of your company. The right person will get extremely excited by this. The wrong person will be turned off and will move on to the next ad. We're a small businesses and don't have the time to answer three hundred different people who respond to the company ad, so it's extremely important to screen the wrong applicants out by including verbiage that will stop them from even applying.

Be sure to focus on competencies and not responsibilities. Don't list things like answering the phone or calling prospects. You want to do a competency list, which are necessary traits in the new hire—for example, being super creative or loving to meet with people.

The very last thing on this very short and clear ad should be a very clear statement inviting them to apply if they consider themselves to be a good fit. In my company, we ask for a resume and a cover letter sent to an email address. It's very simple. We're giving them very clear instructions.

I want to make sure they can follow instructions. This goes for every single one of the positions, and the way I run my business. I'm a leader who does not micromanage. I'm a leader who gives out instructions, and I expect them to be followed to a 'T'. Therefore, I want somebody in my company to come on board and be able to follow my literal instructions. If the instruction is to send a cover letter and resume to this email address, I expect that to be followed through perfectly and those are the only people whose applications I'm going to entertain. First, people who hit reply on the Craigslist ad don't get a response from me because when they send it, it goes to a different email address. I only want people who go specifically to the email I have listed. Second, I'm asking for a resume and a cover letter. If an application comes in without a cover letter, I don't even open it. This is before I actually get to reading it. I'm looking for two different attachments that are sent to a specific email address. If any application doesn't qualify in this, it'll be automatically discarded, because I need somebody in my company and on my team who can follow instructions. This is part of the company culture, how I set the expectations, how I'll move forward, and how I'll manage them or lead them in the future. You must set a tone from the beginning regarding how their experience and their career are going to be within your company. You don't want to let things slide and attract the wrong applicants.

For example, one web development company doesn't take any resumes. They create a page for every job application with four or five questions that really make people think. They don't want people who are lazy and just hit a reply button. They want people who really want the job. At the end of every form there is an optional field saying, "Extra credit: create a quick video cover letter of yourself and post a link here." They're looking for people who go above and beyond, in the same way I'm looking for people who can follow directions. They start by looking at everybody who did the extra credit, and they reach out to those people first. They sometimes never make it down to anybody else, and all the best hires they've ever made have been people who have submitted a video cover letter.

It is important to document your entire hiring process. Keep in mind this question: How would you, as the leader or owner, respond in this situation? What would you do? Go through this process and document every single step of the way. If it's a written response, write it; if it's something you would do, like send a follow-up email, write it down. You're looking for people who think and act like you do. At the end of the day, that's the culture of your company. That's the type of people you want to attract. Don't think about wrong or right; there's no right way or wrong way to do this. There are different ways to do things, and that's fine.

"You want an applicant who will fit your culture, who can think and act like you do, because those are the kind of people who will meet and exceed your expectations."

You're looking for people who fit your culture, who can think and act like you do, because those are the kind of people who will meet and exceed your expectations. If you haven't gone through this process to find out what you would have done, you'll end up with team members who will always fall short of your standards. You won't find the best people for the job. The applicants you find are never going to be good enough for you. They'll never make decisions the way you would, because you didn't hire them the right way and you didn't put in place the right expectations. What's right for your company may not be right for somebody else's company. There are people who have different strengths and different ways of thinking, and they might be completely amazing culture fits for another organization. They are simply not a good culture fit for your organization.

If you document your steps through your own process, you can then scale your hiring process and train your team to do the hiring for you.

If you don't document it, it's nearly impossible to explain to somebody else what you're looking for. You will be limited to hiring everyone yourself. When businesses are small, typically the owners or CEOs hire. But if you document the process it will be in place as you expand. At this point, I enjoy the process, and it empowers me to make sure that we're bringing on the best of the best for our company.

While getting the right person sounds like a lot of work, I don't think there's anything that's more important or has a bigger impact on your organization that having the right team in place.

I firmly believe that all business owners or CEO's of small businesses should focus all of their time on high-priority activities (HPAs). As a small business or as a start-up culture that's looking to double revenue from year to year, nothing has a higher priority than bringing on top-quality talent. This is a process that is ongoing. Once you've filled all the positions in your company— if you've got the right players— they're going to double your business very quickly. That means you're going to need to bring on more top talent.

You need to start looking for people before there's a job opening, or else you'll always have a void. You'll fall short and will stunt your growth goals. This is a process that needs to go on all year for fast-growing businesses. It's a like logistics. If you're a factory, you don't wait for the order to come in to find out who your vendors are. You're always negotiating prices and lining up the next parts because you never know when the demand is going to grow.

After the applicant responds— and follows my exact directions— I move to the next step.

The Initial Response

I send what I call an initial response to the people who followed the instructions I laid out in the ad. I do this before I even open their email attachments. I copy and paste the same text to everybody who makes it through.

It says:

After reviewing your resume and cover letter, I'm interested in learning a little more about you to see if you would be a good fit for our team. Please respond to this email explaining to me how you exemplified each of our company values at your last or current place of employment. Thank you for applying to build a career at our company, and I look forward to hearing from you soon.

Again, this is a critical step, you should complete for yourself first. Write down how you would respond to this email. The funny part is that about 70 percent of people who apply for your position will not respond at all. They don't want to do the work, and you're already weeding them out.

The point of this process is to save your valuable time to only invest on the best applicants. I'm an entrepreneur. My time is very valuable, so I can't interview twenty people for one position, no matter how vital the position. What I am putting in place is a screening technique to make it easy to see very quickly the people who:

- really want this position
- are good fits for our company
- stand out from the other applicants
- are willing to put in the work
- will respond with very similar format and content to the way you would have responded

When I wrote my own "applicant response", I made note of my format. I had a header thanking them for the email. Then I explained how I found each of our company's values. I listed the first one. I underlined it, bolded it, and I wrote a small paragraph about it. I did the same for the next five core values. I had a small paragraph at the end where I thanked them for their time, and I asked for an interview. I closed it up with a "sincerely" and my name.

When I review the applicant's response, I check to see if it visually matches the format of my response. If it is very similar, then that means this person thinks and acts like me. Any responses that don't clearly resemble your response must be screened out. Just because it's an amazing response, that doesn't mean it's the right response. Remember, you want somebody who will be perfectly aligned with your organization and your culture.

Once you've identified the responses that match yours in terms of format, then take a few minutes and read it, looking for content matches. We are looking for applicants that interpret your company's core values in the same way that you interpret them. For example, in our company one of our core values is "lead by excellence." It can mean many different things, but at my company, we describe it in a very particular way. We like being the best. We don't like coming in second place. Everything we do, we do to win. So everybody in my company likes to always get first place. If we get second place, we feel like we lost. We are obsessive about leading by excellence. When we play a game with any of our friends, we get very competitive. We are the people who make sure that we win and that nobody is cheating, because we lead by excellence. This goes for everything we do in our lives. We're looking for people who feel the same way and can describe these values as we do. That's what I mean by checking the content of the response. How did the applicant describe your core values? Did it match your version? Is it aligned with the way that you describe your core values? If there isn't a clear alignment in the content, screen the applicant out.

"To attain the best results and highest probability of success, compare the applicant's response to the way you responded to the ad and the follow-up questions. Look for a near perfect match."

To attain the best results and highest probability of success, you need to design and test your process all the way through, because it's easier to identify unqualified applicants when you've created the way you would react and respond. Put yourself through the system, take notes, and create the baseline for what you're looking for. If you do that little extra work, it's going to be so much easier the next time you start getting resumes.

Again, consider your strengths and how you would respond since you're looking for are people who think like you, act like you, and can make decisions like you would. Take a moment to find some key characteristics within yourself that you can test for during the next few steps.

The Phone Interview

The next step for the people who pass the initial response test is the phone interview. Take the time to set this up properly and it will be one of the strongest screening tools you can use. This step is nonnegotiable at my company and must be followed precisely.

In terms of the timeframe of when to call the chosen candidates, I usually batch all of the calls on one day of the week, unless I'm really excited about somebody based on their response. No more than a week should go by before you call applicants for a phone interview. The quicker you get on the phone with them, the better the response is going to be, and the more excited your candidate will be. If you can do it as soon as the next day, that's great.

I also create a worksheet to keep track of the results of the phone interviews. I place the applicants' names in the first column. The second column is for the quality of their voicemail, so I know who didn't make it through this filter. In the third column, I put the call result so I know if the person is going to call me back or how the call went.

While I schedule time in my day to make the phone interviews, I do not announce to the applicants that I will be making the call.

Reflecting on myself, I know that I get up early in the morning to complete some of my tasks, and I'm pretty thorough with most of the tasks I do because our core value is to lead by excellence. Therefore, I like to do them pretty early in the morning because I'm looking for people who are up early like I am, who are thorough, and who complete a number of tasks early in the day. I want to make sure they're answering their phone calls at this time and that they're busy doing their personal tasks.

If they don't answer the phone call, I listen to their voicemail greeting. What does it sounds like? If the person doesn't have the voice mail activated or the mailbox is full, I mark it in the second column of my worksheet and they are screened out. If I get that person's voice mail, and it doesn't sound similar to my voice mail—a professional message stating my name, maybe even something funny or unique—they don't make it to the next step. It's that simple.

If they do answer the phone, it indicates they are likely to be the right person because they are up early and attentive to their phone—especially if they're in the market and looking for a position. Then I immediately proceed to the phone interview.

When they answer, I say, "Hi. I really enjoyed reading your response to my email, so thank you for taking the time to do that. I wanted to ask you a few basic questions to get know you a little bit better. Do you have some time right now?" Sometimes they say yes and ask for a few minutes to step outside. Other times they may offer to call you back at a different time, and that's perfectly fine. Most of the time, the right person will immediately take my call because I'm a potential employer and he's excited about the ad and about the position. He took the time to write a response, so he's eager for the call and the job.

"The right person will immediately take my early morning call. He took the time to write a response, so he's eager for the call and the job."

I then ask four questions in the phone interview— easy questions that make the process faster.

The first question: "What are your long-term goals? What are you going to be doing five years from now?" I'm looking for people who have some type of goals that are in line with the future direction of our company or in line with how our company operates. Remember that millennials don't really plan this far out into the future, so don't expect these answers to be fully thought out and/or well explained at this point. Also, it's not necessarily a bad thing if the candidate has a tough time answering this question.

A lot of times, the answer you receive may be in your company's current field, but when it comes to millennials, mostly you're going to get some kind of entrepreneurial mind-set response. A lot of them give you answers like "I'd like to own my own business" or "I'd like to be in a leadership position." They may list certain things about your company that they like, because the right person would have done his research and know about your industry. You want to listen to them and hear how they speak.

Your goal with this question is to weed out somebody who is completely misaligned with your goals or the growth and the impact of your company. Someone who isn't clear on what you do and what your company wants to achieve is also a misfit. You also want to avoid somebody who doesn't have any goals. If the candidate is completely misaligned, simply screen them out, end the call politely, and take the candidate out of your pipeline.

The second question: "What are a couple of things that you are the best at doing?" This is the person's time to brag. It's the easiest question they are going to get, and usually they have no problem with talking about the things that they consider themselves to be really good at. If the candidate lists too many things, ask what things he or she thinks they are better at than all of their friends? This way you'll reduce the list. I normally like to limit it to three to five things. Write these things down. What you're looking for here are three things that reveal their personal core competencies. You're looking for people who have strengths that align with the things that are required for the position. This will help you get a higher probability of success for this person in that position.

You would think that people would remember what your job posting ad said and give you the answer that they think you would want to hear, but in my experience that's not true. They don't really remember the ad and they truthfully tell you what they're really good at doing. They enjoy this question, so let them speak, take notes, and write down as much as you can.

> **"You would think that people would remember what your job posting ad said and give you the answers they think you want to hear, but they don't. They truthfully tell you what they're really good at doing."**

The third question brings up the flip side: "What are the things that you're really, really not good at doing?" This is the toughest part of the phone interview. Only a few will answer this question quickly and start talking without hesitation. Why? Because it's a very difficult question. You're asking about their weaknesses. Most candidates will start to give you a traditional response first, the answer that they've trained for in school or with friends or peers. The first response you're going to get is something along the lines of them being perfectionists or too organized. "People tell me that I spend most of my time organizing, so I am a perfectionist." You're going to get these answers a lot. When you get these responses, tell them point-blank that sounds like a strength. Then ask them again what they are not good at. "I'm looking for a real weakness."

They're going to change their tone a little. They know you're serious about the question. This is a critical; you need to push to get the weaknesses out of this person. There are a couple of things I'm screening for. First, if you push and still don't get any weaknesses, you end the call, screen this candidate out and move on. Anybody who feels that he's perfect and doesn't have any flaws is probably not a good fit for your team. I need people who are mature enough to know that there are some things that they're just not very good at doing.

You can push in different ways, like rewording the question. A way to reword it could be something like, "The next step in the hiring process involves me setting up a few calls with some of your supervisors from some of your previous employments. One of the questions I'm going to ask them is to tell me the things that they felt you were not good at doing. When I speak to them, what answers do you think that they are going to tell me?"

The fear of the reference check is apparent here. I really want to know their weaknesses, and if they don't tell me, I'm going to find somebody else who will. At this point, they're going to open up to you, and they're going to tell you a few of their weaknesses. Some people will not be startled and say, "Well, I don't think they're going to say anything. I think everybody was happy with my work, and I don't think there's anything that I wasn't good at."

Then you can try and reword this question once more. I do this if I'm really trying to get something from them before I screen out the candidate. I ask people to tell me a few things that they're not interested in doing professionally. For example, if you're hiring for a creative director position, this type of person will probably not be interested in organizing the finances for your company. They'll say, "I'm not interested in finances. I'm not interested in putting together financial reports. I'm not interested in organizing budgets." Those are valid, perfect responses. When you're a creative director for a marketing company, you don't want the person to do any of these tasks. You're also listening for some other things you're okay with accepting about this person. However, if one of the weaknesses somehow violates the core competencies needed for this position, then you will screen out this person for that position.

> **"If one of your applicant's weaknesses violates a core competency needed for your position, screen them out of this job. However, if they are a good cultural fit, consider placing them in another spot"**

Write down these weaknesses and make certain they are not something that will impair this person from being successful in the position they have applied for. For example, if you're looking for a public relations director and this person has a weakness in communicating with people. Some of the responses will be obvious like that and some responses less so.

People may culturally fit your organization, but their core competencies don't align with this position. There's a difference between teachable skills and core competencies— like creativity or logic, that typically cannot be taught. If you really like this person and they sound like a perfect fit for your culture, perhaps this is not the right position for them. You may keep them in the pipeline for another position.

The fourth question asks several sub-questions about their resume and requests contact information for their previous supervisors. Start by referring to their most recent position listed on their resume. Ask: "What was the name and position of your former supervisor?" Here is a little tip to keep your candidates honest and stop them from bluffing. When you ask for the name of the previous supervisor, ask them to spell out the last or the first name— to make sure you get it right. When you ask them to spell it, they'll know you're writing it down and they'll know you're going to talk to this person. It's important you do this before you start asking the rest of the questions, because you want to get truthful answers.

Next questions: "What was the reason for leaving the position?"

Then: "When I speak to your former supervisor and ask them to rate your performance on a scale of one to ten, with one being this was the worst employee they've ever had and ten being this was the best person to ever work for this company, what number do you think they'll tell me?"

The correct way to ask this question to get the most truthful response is: "When I call Mr. Martinez from XYZ Company, and I ask him to rate your performance during your time there on a scale of one to ten, what number do you think Mr. Martinez is going to tell me?" People are going to give you a number. Here is your key to this. If you get a response of a ten or a nine, it's a great score, which means that this person did well. An eight is a neutral score, and a seven or below will tell you that there was a problem with this person at this position.

I recommend you go through at least the last three to five jobs in this manner. The important part is that you go through as much as you can. I don't care if it's six or seven years ago—I go through all of them. We're looking for things that stand out, for things that maybe candidates didn't put in the resume or won't mention in the typical interview, and real reasons why they left previous positions. Try to understand the character of the candidate, any potential trends or habits about the candidate, and how they view or think about themselves.

Most of the time you're going to see the right people giving themselves nines and tens; those are usually great employees. If they give themselves a grade that's low, chances are there was some kind of problem in that company. If they give me a seven or below, I usually ask, "Why do you think it was not a ten?" Have the candidates tell you their side of the story and write it down. I verify this information during the reference check stage.

Before we end the call, I tell people that the next step involves me speaking to the references they mentioned during the call. Once I speak to them and everything checks out exactly with the information that they provided me, then I will give them a callback, or I'll reach out to them to schedule a face-to-face interview. Ask the candidate to email you with the best contact information for the supervisors or coworkers they mentioned during the phone interview. Make sure you go back and list the names of each of the references and then end the call.

> **"Too many managers don't respect themselves enough to immediately end the hiring process at any step because they feel it's disrespectful of the candidate. It's more disrespectful to waste a person's time, knowing there's no chance we will work together."**

If after any of the questions—even after the first one—you sense that this person is not the best fit, feel free to end the call. If you don't get a good alignment or if there's an obvious disconnect, end the call. At question number two, the strengths, if you get a misalignment, politely excuse yourself and end the call. For question number three, if they don't want to give you any straight answers, or there are some weaknesses that contradict with what the competencies needed for the position are, end the call. This way you only go through the entire call with the people who could actually be a great fit. A complete phone call like this lasts about fifteen minutes; however, I normally get calls completed in five to seven minutes. Our time is valuable. Don't waste it once it becomes clear there will be no future work relationship with this applicant. Too many managers don't respect themselves enough to immediately end the hiring process at any step because they feel it's disrespectful of the candidate. I think it's much more disrespectful for a person to waste my time, knowing that there is no chance we are going to work together.

The Reference Checks

At the end of the phone interview, you left the candidate with clear instructions. You told them that the next step is for them to send you the best contact information for each of the previous managers you spoke about. And, very importantly, you listed the names to them verbally so they know exactly who you're looking for. Then you tell them, "As soon as you I get in contact with all of these people, they corroborate everything that we've spoken about today, and I don't get any surprises based on the conversation we had today, I'll be reaching out to you again to schedule a face-to-face interview." This is how the call ends. At this point, nothing further will happen with this candidate until the email is received. This means we will not follow-up with the candidate ever again unless we receive their email with the best contact info for each reference. Also, any deviations from these clear instructions will disqualify the candidate. Regardless of how amazing this candidate may have been up to this point, we must resist the temptation to bend or break this rule in the process.

You asked the candidate to give you the best contact information—that was the instruction. What's going to happen from here is that the true leaders will normally get you this information very quickly. Your true rock stars might get it to you within an hour or two. However, just because the candidate doesn't give it to you that quickly, does not mean that they are not a true rock star. I have found that sometimes there are multiple layers that the candidate must go through to find the correct contact information. Additionally, some of the best candidates like to ask permission from their references before giving out their personal phone numbers. I'm sure we can all understand this.

"Be wary if an applicant gives you general company phone numbers or emails instead of direct or personal phone numbers for references. In my experience this is usually a bad sign."

Be wary if you get general company phone numbers or emails instead of phone numbers. In my experience this is usually a bad sign. It's not to say that it can't lead to something positive, but in my experience, 90 percent of the time they want to hide something and stop you from accessing that person. Maybe 25–30 percent of your candidates will never send you the list, which is kind of odd, don't you think?

Again, that's a clear indication they have something to hide. Resist the temptation to follow-up with the candidate.

Once you receive the email, look for two things: excellent contact numbers, and the speed with which they send them to you. Ideally, their contacts' information should be direct lines and/or cell phone numbers. The phone numbers should let you access people quickly. You'll just ask a few questions on these phone calls, almost like the questions you asked the candidate. My typical phone call starts like this:

Hey, Mr. Smith, my name is Javier, I'm calling because I had [candidate name] apply for a position with our company. I was wondering if you could give me some quick personal feedback on your experience while working with [candidate name]. I have three questions I want to ask you about this person and your personal interaction during their time with you at [previous company name].

Most of the time, people will be very helpful, especially if it's a positive reference. People genuinely want to help the candidate out, so you can get right to it. The key to this is to be friendly. Coming across overly formal or professional tends to intimidate and scare references from being honest and open with you. Be natural and comfortable so you make them feel comfortable. Then they can give you the real, honest answers. Ask easy questions.

The first question: "On a scale of one to ten, with one being the worst employee I ever had and ten being the most amazing person you have ever worked with, how would you rate this person's performance during his/her time with you?"

If the person is beating around the bush, press a little harder to make sure that they give you one number, not a range. This is vital because the same rule I mentioned before applies here. Nines and tens means this person was great, eight is a neutral number, and seven and below typically means there was a problem with this person.

If you get the nines and tens, great; there's no need to dive really much deeper. With nines and tens, most people are going to offer you other information to support their decision for that number, so you're not going to have to probe too much. When you get an eight or below, people are usually a bit quieter, and you will most likely need to probe a little more.

Now, I wouldn't probe just yet. Take the number they give you and move on to the next question, just to give them a sense that this is going to be a very quick phone call and you're not going to take up too much of their time.

The next question: "Would you please tell me a few things that this person was truly the very best at doing." Take notes about what they tell you and move on. And the follow-up question asks the flip side: "Would you please tell me a few things that this person was honestly, truly not good at doing?" With true rock stars, most of the times these references are going to tell you that they were really good at everything and fun to have around. That's fine, but you should probably do some probing to get at least one answer. Or you might want to reword the question for them. "Okay, I understand they were really good at everything that they were scheduled to do, but was there something that they maybe weren't really interested in doing, or maybe something that they could've used a little help to do a bit better?" You're looking for weaknesses; you're looking for something lacking that the supervisor or coworker felt the person could have improved upon.

The last question: "If the opportunity arose again, would you consider this person for rehire?" Again, if people are getting nines and tens, chances are bosses are going to say yes. So that's pretty much it.

At this point, if the person rated the candidate a seven or below, I always say, "So you rated this person seven. Why did this person not get a nine or a ten?" Don't ask, "Why did they get a 7?" People don't know how to answer that. If you ask, "Why did you not give them a nine or ten?"

or "What were they missing to get to a nine or ten?" you're going to get a true, honest answer about the reasons and the problems. Sometimes they'll get down to the nitty-gritty and be specific. Other times they'll beat around the bush — but you'll still get a good inkling into what happened, what weakness this person had, and why he or she didn't score higher than a seven.

It's a really good question, and you want to ease the tension off this reference person, because the moment people get tense, they're going to close up, give you short answers, and end the call as soon as they can. Make it very easy for them, and make them very comfortable. In today's world, everyone is so terrified of receiving a lawsuit or being accusing of defaming a person. So it's truly important that you approach and ask these questions in the friendliest and most comfortable way, so that you can get true answers.

"A key question to ask references: 'Is there anything else you want me to know about this person before we hang up?'"

Just before I hang up—and I find that this reveals unexpected information—I say, "Okay, great. Those are all the questions I have. Thank you very much for your time. Is there anything else you want me to know about this person before we hang up?" At this time, manager or coworker will usually open up. They'll tell you a couple of extra good things about the candidate… or maybe a couple of extra bad things about this person that weren't prompted by the questions you had scheduled. Perhaps they wanted to get some things off their chest, but you didn't really take them that direction. Asking people this question opens the door and says, "Hey, tell me anything else you want me to know about this person."

You'll get a little bit more insight. Again, with the rock stars that are scoring nines and tens, most of the times when you get to this question, there will not be much added because this person has already talked the world about the candidate. But every now and then, you're going to get sevens or lower and these are red flags. Now you really want to dive deeper and see if, through the interactions you've had with this person, you're finding a common trend.

Humans are creatures of habits and tend to repeat themselves. Talking with different references lets you see different experiences that they've had with different companies at which they've worked. That will give you good insight into that person. Everybody can be a rock star for the right company. You want to determine: "Does this person fit the mold for my culture? Does this person have the right mind-set, skill set, and competencies for what I'm looking for?" Search for weaknesses. You want to check them against your competencies for the position and compare them to the candidate. If you start hearing things during the reference check that are weaknesses that strongly work against what this position's main tasks are going to be, it should raise some concerns for you. It's something for you to talk about when you bring that person in for the face-to-face interview, if you decide you want to do that. Otherwise, you want the person to have weaknesses that will not affect their performance in the position they are applying for or in the culture of your company.

When the candidates are young and fresh out of high school or college, I look for volunteer or internship experience. If they don't have that, you may want to ask for professors as references. You need a list of people to talk with as a part of the reference check so you can ask about their personal experience with the candidate. Top candidates will stand out and will offer you options. Even if they've done absolutely nothing that they can put on their resume, they're going to tell you, "Well, I had a babysitting job back when I was fifteen, and I could put you in contact with that person." A rock star will typically offer you solutions to these problems. If the person is very closed and says he never had any work and doesn't have anybody he can give you as a reference, that is likely a red flag. I would probably pass on that candidate.

You may need to search and get creative. If they've only had one job, ask for other people who worked at that company and are no longer there, but who might have interacted with them (ideally in a supervisory role). They may have been at a previous company for ten years, and it may be the only job they've ever had. That's fine. Just be sure to talk to at least three different people there.

"How did your young candidate fill their free time? Top candidates do productive things such as volunteering, sports, or other activities. Look for a background that shows he or she is a rock star, even if it's not in the professional world."

If they haven't had a lot of working experience, then they must have had some free time, and top candidates would've filled that with productive things such as volunteering, sports, or other activities. Look for somebody whose background shows that he or she is a rock star, even if it's not in the professional world.

For example, if the activity is a sport, talk to the coach, who can you give you feedback on the person. "What's this person really, really good at?" "She's great at motivating the team. She inspires people. She was great at showing up for practice on time. She was very dedicated and never missed a practice." All this information gives insight into this person.

Once the person makes it through the initial response test, the phone interview, and the reference checks they've earned the right to impose on your schedule. Now you're going to take some of your very valuable and limited time and schedule a face-to-face interview.

The Face-to-Face Interview

Very few people make it this far because you've screened out a lot of unsuitable candidates. The way I present a face-to-face interview is very simple. I normally email the candidate and say, "Congratulations. I've spoken to all your references, and I'd like to meet with you face-to-face." Usually, I give people two or three options of times and dates that would work well for them to come into our office. I usually get a prompt response.

While you're confirming the face-to-face interview, our company gives people a very clear task, something simple they can do. For example, you could ask people to bring you two copies of their cover letter and three copies of their resume. Be very clear and specific, and see how well they follow the instructions. Feel free to get creative with the task. It's only important that we make sure the task is clear and that the candidate can easily execute it. Another example could be: "When you arrive, please make sure that you park in the 3rd parking space from the left." Little things like that will help you see how well the candidate can follow directions that are given them.

If people don't do these simple tasks and bring one copy instead of three, but they did everything else right—they showed up on time, dressed professionally, et cetera—I would probably see them. But it's a strike against them. Now, other things are nonnegotiable. For example, if you don't show up early for the interview, you won't even get invited in. This is not acceptable in my company. Other companies might not see that as a problem, because it's not a core competency for their culture. That's fine. But in our company, we don't tolerate being late to an appointment.

Every company has its own standards. Know the non-negotiables in your organization. During the face-to-face interview, I also try to put candidates through a small test to see how they would react to the environment their job entails. If it's an operations person, I try to make the interview very much like an operational environment; driven by systems and processes.

If you're hiring for sales (which is one of the hardest positions for entrepreneurs to hire effectively), the interview is a complete sales experience for this person and for you. Sales is the easiest hiring situation for me to explain and one you can probably relate with, so I will give an example of a sales interview, first. When a sales candidate comes in for the interview, they are selling themselves on why we should hire them. The interview itself is an example of their best sales presentation.

While scheduling the interview with the candidate, I present the interview as follows, "This entire interview will be an audition. Please go on our website and familiarize yourself with some of our products, because I will ask you to sell a product to me, and I want to see what your sales experience is." This is a twofold instruction. I'm disguising what I'm really saying in the question. I'm telling them that the entire interview will be an audition, which is very important—it's key. Then I'm disguising it by saying, "Go on our website and learn one of our products, because I'm going to ask you sell it to me."

I also tell them, "I don't expect you to know the complete ins and outs of all of our products, so don't worry about all the details. I just want you to have a basic understanding of what our company sells so that you can sell our product a little better."

When people come in for the interview, they are trying to sell themselves because I told them the entire interview is an audition. They treat me like a customer and, as a customer, I am interested in buying. But the candidates are selling the thing closest to them, themselves. They are going to do the best job they possibly can. People will come in wearing their best dress clothes. They'll show up at the best time they know and deliver everything the best they can. They will never be able to sell anything, including your products, better than they are going to be able to sell themselves. They're never going to have more motivation to sell your products, than to sell themselves.

"If people can't sell themselves, they are not going to be able to sell your product or service."

If people can't sell themselves, they are not going to be able to sell your product or service. They believe in themselves. They know themselves better than anything else. They have the most to gain from making this sale. Understand the mind-set of the candidate. I'm telling you that they're going to do the very best they know how to do. They're not going to do 70 percent because they're the ones with the vested interest in making this sale, and that is getting the job.

When you bring them in, treat them like one of your toughest clients treats you. Think about what this person's job will be and the kind of rejection they'll get from your prospective clients when they start selling your products. More often than not, the potential clients they call will not be interested in their offer, regardless of how friendly they are on the phone. Your applicant has to face rejection and be okay with it. Want to see how they are going to react when trying to make sales for you or networking for you? Test them at your interview as they try to sell themselves.

When they arrive at my office, I'm going to act like a client and let them wait in the waiting room. Normally I won't greet them; I have somebody in my office greet them and have them sit in the waiting room and anxiously wait for me. Why do I do that? Because when they go to meet your clients, most of the time they're going to think like, "I'm nervous already. What if the client doesn't like me or won't want to work with me?" It's a little bit intimidating, and this interview should feel the same way.

Five to six minutes later, I walk over to the waiting room, say, "Hi." I pause for a second, then say, "Follow me." I'll be a bit dry, a little rude, act uninterested, and I don't shake hands. I simply direct them to come to the back room with me.

It's an act, a drama. This is a rough process for them. But this is how my toughest clients will treat them. If they can't handle this and don't do well under pressure, then they're probably not going to do well interviewing for me or working with my clients.

I take them to the office and we sit down. I start with the basic question: "Why do you want this job?" Again, I'm being dry, cutthroat, and rough with them. They usually start talking and rambling and I listen to see how well they react to my unfriendliness.

In the best sales process, the salesperson needs to assess and act right from the beginning. Ideally, the person tries to build rapport with me, so he should start off with small talk. He should try to get through to this tough guy who's in front of him. If the applicant doesn't do this, that's fine; this is still an interview. Most of the time, the applicant tends to back out a little bit, not be too forthcoming, and try and come at you from all directions. This is an indication of how they'll act with your clients.

Once they give an answer, I say, "Well, all right. Let's get right to it. Do me a favor. I want you to sell one of our products to me. Pick any one of our products you like. Actually, you know what? Pick this product." I'll pick a product for them and say, "Sell me this product. Ready? Let's do it." We start the sales process. They're very nervous at this point; their hearts are beating fast and they start sweating. Most of the people who come to work for my company have never sold before. They don't really know anything about sales. They just googled a little about sales presentations, learned some things about our company, and spent a bit of time researching the industry.

Most of the time applicants don't do well with the sales presentation. Every now and then, we get a very good salesperson who knocks it out of the park. She presents it very well, asks a lot of questions, and does things that an experienced sales person would do. But applicants who go through this rigorous hiring process are so nervous that they don't do well. When they seem to get to the end of their presentation, you assess how well they did. This is a very tough part. I will look at them and say, "Okay, let's just stop right there. This is not going to be a good fit for us. Thank you for your time." I will stand up as if I'm leaving out the door, and if they haven't done it already, I open the door and ask them to leave.

I know a salesperson should never let a sale go without understanding why the person is not buying. This is another way I assess their experience in sales. They should always ask why. It's a very difficult thing to do, especially in an interview when you've put in your total effort and somebody is walking you out. You get nervous, but you just have to follow it. Again, almost everyone fails this part.

> **"The applicant is stunned and confused. They just got rejected and were leaving… and now I'm asking them to come back into the office. Now I can coach and lead them."**

This is a very uncomfortable situation. That's perfectly fine. If this person has really knocked it out of the park with everything else, and I think he's a good fit, and I like this person, I do something different. As he's walking out the door, I stop and say, "All right. You know what? Let's stop all this. Come back in, and let's just have a seat and talk." Now the applicant is stunned and confused by what's happening. They just got totally rejected and were leaving… and now I'm asking them to come back into the office.

I sit down with them and say, "All right, so, let's talk about what happened." I explain everything to them. Everything. I say:

I told you over the phone this entire thing was going to be an audition. You don't have sales experience, but you're here to sell yourself. If you're going to sell yourself, and I told you you're not going to be a good fit, you should always ask to understand why. How can you just walk out of here with no understanding why you didn't get the job? You've gone through this entire process. You're excited about this position, you want to be part of this company, and this is your opportunity—and I'm telling you no. How can you get up and walk away so easily? I want you to understand that if you work for our company, and if you fail at any sales presentation and the customer tells you no, the first thing I'm going to ask you about your sales presentation is to tell me why. If you can't answer that question, we're going to have a problem because we can't grow as an organization from that type of feedback. It's impossible for us to get any better if you don't do this.

Now, I'm teaching, coaching, and developing the millennial who's sitting in front of me. Interviewees are getting firsthand experience about what it's like to work for our company. They see how invested I'm going to be in coaching, developing, and training them. I don't care how full of themselves or how confident they are. I just broke them to such a low level and now I'm going to build them up and help them grow from this point forward.

Typically, at this point millennials think, "I thought I was really good. I thought I really knew about sales, and I was very confident because at every single job I've been to, I was a rock star." All job seekers think they are a rock star. Now, all of a sudden they've realized, "Wait a second. I don't know everything, and there's a lot for me to learn. This person sitting in front of me could be my future leader. He's going to teach me and invest time into coaching me. I'll learn something new and better my skills." As we mentioned before, millennials look for new opportunities to learn and be coached in their workplace. You're interviewing them, but you're also giving them insight into the value of working here and what we'll do for them as individuals.

While millennials seek this kind of leadership, they simply can't see it everywhere, and they don't know how committed a company really is to developing them. In my company, they will get firsthand experience with many new concepts and learn a lot. We're going to be very invested in every member on our team.

That's why I go through this very long process. I want to make sure I have the right person before I invest time developing them. The person sitting across from me, who's here considering working for my company, now starts to get a glimpse of what it will be like in our culture. They see the opportunity to be challenged and developed on a daily basis.

Of course, you don't only have salespeople in your company. Every position is going to be a little bit different, so you have to determine what will be the toughest part of that role for this person. Whatever it is, I'll try to recreate that exact situation. For example, answering phones, phone rejections, or getting questions on leads, or how they turn that lead and convert it. I'm going to try to put them in a scenario where I can let them know that there's going to be a lot more to it than they anticipated, and our team has a lot of value to teach them. I break them down and essentially say, "Hey, you're not as good as you think you are, and there's a lot to learn. We can teach you here." The top performing millennials will crave that kind of leadership.

For example, let's take an operations person. I typically start off by asking organizational core competency questions. In my opinion, an operations person should be very organized and very disciplined. An operations person should have a lot of work figured out and done in advance. An operations person is also very detail oriented, especially when it comes to scheduling. If we're considering a candidate for an operations role, the first thing I ask when leading the interview is "All right, how do you organize your typical day?"

The person might say, "I organize my day in a calendar, and I write everything down."

"Okay, where's your calendar?"

"Well, I have it in my car. I have it here, or I have it at home."

If they have it around there, I'm going to ask them for the calendar. I want to see how long the calendar is. I want to see how they are organizing their activities every day. I'm really pushing it to call their bluff.

They may say, "My calendar is on my phone."

"Show me your calendar on your phone. I'd like to see how you organize all your activities and appointments." The right people will have this down perfectly and be very proud to show it to you. An extremely organized person always has their calendar with them.

They could say, "This is how I organize all my appointments, but I left my calendar at home." This is a red flag for you. How does a person organize his day and leave his calendar at home? If I sat here right now and said, "Hey, let's meet next week. I want you to come in, and I'm going to give you the job. I want you to start on Tuesday at 9:00 a.m.," this person should be able to readily pull out his calendar and tell you if he's available. It's impossible that somebody is that organized and leaves his calendar at home. That calendar should never leave the person's side. At the very least, it should be sitting in his car.

Most of the time, especially with millennials, it's going to be on their phone. They'll have the phone either with them, or in the car. If it's in their car, I ask them to get it for me. Most of the time they do come back in. The ones who were lying to me—and it's happened to me twice—tell me that the cell phone battery is dead, or never even come back into the office. Red flag.

On their calendar, I look for how they organize all of their appointments and whether they have set repetitive events. A really strong operations person is very habitual about how he organizes his day. Are there certain things they do every single day? Are there certain things they do multiple times a week?"

Most operationally-driven people are typically into exercising, in my experience. Ask them when they go to the gym. Any really good operations person goes to the gym at the exact same time on the exact same days. They may tell you, "I go every morning at six," or "I go Monday, Wednesday, and Friday at 10:00 a.m." This is how they naturally live their lives— disciplined and organized. Anything outside of that would make them uncomfortable.

If they answer, "I go whenever I have time," this will not be a good candidate for an operations position. If the answer is anything along a systematically scheduled time, then you know you have a good fit. This person will tell you about his routine—times, days, dates. You really want to see what the role of this person is going to be. What does this person need to have in order to be successful in this position? You want to start checking him against these competencies during this face-to-face interview.

I normally stay away from the traditional interview questions, because they have no value to me. I want to meet the people and get to know them better. Are they as amazing in person as they sounded over the phone? Are they as sharp as I need them to be? Are they as likable? Do they feel as comfortable as I expect them to be? I test them based on the position I need to fill. I want to see if they have the core competencies that this position needs. Do they really fall in line with our core values?" Basically, I verify everything they've said up until this point and then delve deeper.

At the end of the interview, my goal is to show people that there's a lot of value and knowledge to be learned here. I show them I'm willing to work with them and teach them. At some point, I will refer to the values in the organization and expect them to be familiar with them and understand how important they are to our organization.

"Our company values are the reason for every decision we make, including hiring and firing. If they violate any one of our core values, that's immediate grounds for termination. There's no three-strike rule in our company."

I also explain to them that our company values are the reason for every decision we make, including hiring and firing. If they violate any one of our core values at any point in our company, that's immediate grounds for termination. There's no three-strike rule in our company. I explain this at the interview, so they know what the culture is and what's it going to be like.

A couple of things are accomplished when they come into the office: they step into the environment and I get to see how the applicant fits into our environment. They get to see the culture and see our values on the wall. They feel the atmosphere. They begin to get a sense of what this company will be like to work for. You see if the applicant will fit in well to the company and the culture. This is one of the most powerful takeaways of the face-to-face interview. If at any point during this interview, you feel that this person is not going to be a good fit for your culture, screen the candidate out and end the interview. My interviews tend to last anywhere between forty-five to sixty minutes.

At the close of the interview I normally say:

Well, I think that's all the questions I have for today. I really enjoyed meeting you. I want you to go home and digest all the information you've gotten today. I know we talked a lot and we experienced a lot together. I want you to take at least twenty-four hours to survey all of it and let it all sink in. After that, I want you to send me an email telling me where you are, what you're thinking, what you're feeling, and any particular comments or thoughts that you might have on whether this company's going to be right for you.

There are two critical pieces in this message. One, I give instructions not to send this email within the next ten minutes. I'm testing again. Will they continuing to follow the instructions I give them? Two, I'm giving them time to digest everything and let it soak in, because they've just gotten a boat load of information to process.

Sometimes a candidate says, "I don't need twenty-four hours—I'm in." But more often than not, people (especially the true rock stars) follow directions very well. The ones I hired typically tell me the same thing: they knew exactly how they felt right away, but I told them to wait a little bit, so they did. Most of the time, they'll follow directions; they don't jump out of their seats and say, "I'm in!" But I'm pretty sure they're excited and pumped up.

The reason you don't tell them to send you the email right away is because some of these people are interview professionals. They have it down to a science. They go straight home and send their prewritten email. When you ask them to tell about their experience and what their thoughts are, they have to sit there and write that email. They can't just say, "Thank you for your time, it was really nice meeting you. I look forward to talking about the next steps." This email doesn't answer your questions. When you force them to take time, they're going to be honest with you in this email. They want you to know their thought and feelings. They're willing to share their pulse.

There's another byproduct of this process. Since you've shown them they're not as good as they thought they were, they will be more accepting of a lower offer. This is because their ego is not where it was when they started the application process with your organization.

Typically, you'll get an email the next day, or maybe a day after, that says three things: how excited they are, how much they learned from the experience, and a question about the next step of the process. Most people find good reasons to feel excited about working at your company. Every now and then, someone will say, "Thank you for your time, but this really isn't for me." Perhaps they didn't get along with you or didn't connect with your office atmosphere. That's fine. That's the point of all this. You want to only work with the people who are a good fit for your culture and are sure they want to be part of your company for the long term.

You need to have them reach out to you with a clear and concise decision. The next step is up to them. If you don't hear from them, move on. No follow-up means they'll treat your customers the exact same way.

Trial Day

Once you get the email, it usually means that this person is going to be a great fit. The next step is to schedule a trial date at the office. I tell them, "I'd really like to work with you. We're excited about bringing you on to our team. The next step in the hiring process is for you to spend a few hours here at our office learning about our company and the team members. This is to see whether our company is truly going to be a good fit for you and for us."

Your applicant might be working full-time when they switch to your company, so they are not as available as somebody who's not working. However, we're only asking for four to six hours, so typically we can do a half day. No one has ever refused. At this point, the person is really serious about securing a position with your company. Sometimes people tell us that they can't schedule on a specific day because they want to let their company know.

On trial day, invite them to come in and really interact with the members of your team. You may have them spend all their time the department with their direct reports. Or you can take them around and introduce them one-by-one to every person on your team.

"Trial day is not about teaching the candidate. It's about your team. You want to see how your team feels about this person being a good fit for your culture."

Before the trial day starts, pre-instruct your team. Tell them this applicant is coming in to spend a few hours with them. This is not about teaching the candidate. It's about your team. You want to see how your team feels about this person being a good fit for your culture. Explain this to your team before this trail day begins. They'll spend time talking about their roles and having the applicant shadow them. But the goal is to have your team engage with this person. At the end of the day, you will ask each of them to give you feedback about how they feel the candidate will fit into our culture.

During the first three hours, the candidate is going to be guarded. The third, fourth, and fifth hours are the ones where the person comes out of her shell and becomes more comfortable. Now you begin to see how well they mesh with your team… or not. Let me repeat. This day is only a shadowing day, where candidates sit next to each one of your team members. Again, if it's a bigger company, they may only interact within the department in which they will be working. Sit them down with different people and let each person explain a little bit about the company. You want the candidates to see the culture, learn the rules and internal functions, and understand what each position does and is responsible for. They gain insight into the office atmosphere because they spend most of the day here. They see what a typical day at your company is run like and they get to sit down and interact with the people with whom they're going to be working with every day.

The trial day will solidify everything that you've done up until this point. It will confirm 100 percent if your candidate is a perfect fit for your culture. As the leader, at the end of this day, talk with them privately about their experience from the day. I make it very casual, asking about what they liked, what they learned, and what was their overall impression. The idea is to get a one-on-one pulse in an atmosphere much more relaxed than the interview. At the end of the conversation, you tell the candidate that you'll be in touch over the next few days, and the meeting is over.

The most important part of the day is after the candidate leaves. Now you pull the team together and ask them to rate candidates against each one of your company values, noting how well or how poorly they felt that the candidate did. It's not a performance-based rating—what you're really asking is whether the candidate is a good cultural fit. I usually end this meeting by ask them each directly, "Do you think this person is a good fit for our culture? Yes or no?"

That will give you a lot of insight on how your team truly feels.

The Offer

If you and your team are happy about the candidate after their trial day, the next step is presenting an offer. I normally email the person and say, "Thank you for coming in for the trial day. I'd like to meet with you for lunch, because I'm ready to make an offer to you and I want to present it to you in person." Then we schedule a time to meet for lunch.

Always keep in mind a typical millennial, is motivated by success and by dreaming about a better future. I pick a place to go for lunch that's a little bit nicer than average. I want a place where they have a great outside-the-box experience. I hope I will give this person a sense of, "This is what success is going to be like. This is what the future is going to be like when you're with us. This is how great things are after you've succeeded with us."

At lunch, we talk about the position and then go over an offer. I explain what's expected of them. For example, for a salesperson, I'm going to break down exactly what that person is expected to do in their first twelve months in terms of production. During this meeting, it's imperative that we clearly define what success looks like for them and how we will be rating their performance.

I always recommend bringing a printout clearly explaining how their pay will be structured. This gives them a visual as you present the offer. Break it down for your new hire in very easy and very simple manner. If you have anything based on incentive, it's important that you break it down into details and give examples. "This is your basic salary. This is what you get in commissions, and this is what you get in bonuses." Millennials need to see what their deliverables are going to be within the first twelve months and the results that must be achieved to attain said bonuses, commissions, etc.

You don't say, "At the end of this year, what I expect you to do is …" You need to go into detail. My presentation of the offer for a salesperson sounds something like: "This is what's expected of you over the twelve months after your hiring date. It's been done before, and it's what the minimum standard is. I wanted to present these numbers to you because I want you to understand these are the minimums I want you to achieve. You should aim to exceed these numbers. Assuming that you hit these goals and these minimums that I'm setting for you, your base compensation will be $45,000. When you achieve the minimum of $1 million in sales, commission will look like this." Then I break down the commission. "Let's say the commission is 5 percent of the million dollars. That is $50,000, plus your base pay. That would give you a total annual pay of $95,000." Then you break it down for them into a two-week gross pay check amount. "Therefore, your average two-week gross pay check for your first 12 months will be about $3,653.85." Of course, all of these numbers are made up for the purposes of this example. The important thing is to understand to what detail the offer should be broken down.

This is how millennials process information. You're teaching them that this is what success looks like, as well as what's expected of them. If they reach the minimums set for them, this is what's going to be their annual pay that they're going to make during their first twelve months with you, and what their average check will be. That is how millennials are used to thinking. They come with the mind-set of an hourly rate, a dollar amount that they see on their checks very 2 weeks. You've got to paint the picture for them, especially for a sales position, because it is very hard for them to understand that when they start this new position with you, they're not going to get that average check. But once they start to get the ball rolling, closing their sales, down the line their checks are going to be higher. What you're explaining is the average of all the checks put together, because at the end of the twelve months, they're going to make, say, $95,000, and that translates into an average check of this specific amount.

This is how millennials will understand it best. This gets them optimistic about the future and excited about what they're working toward. You're setting up their expectations from day one. They hear $95,000, which is a lot of money, and that's great! But at the same time, you're letting them know clearly what you expect them to do in exchange for that. Anything less is not going to end well.

Then I normally add a couple of different perks, like mentioning that after their first ninety days, they have unlimited vacation time, and that you have no set office hours. Always connecting it back to what is expected of them. "This is what's expected of you. So if you want to take three months off, take three months off—but you're being held accountable for these numbers at the end of your first year." You should clearly convey the message, "This is how it's going to be. That's final." Once they know what success looks like, they need a clearly defined plan how to get there, and that's what the offer spells out.

> **"Once they know what success looks like, they
> need a clearly defined plan how to get there,
> and that's what the offer spells out."**

I usually have a printed one-sheet presentation of the offer for them. I would say 50 percent of the people accept it right then and there. The other 50 percent take it home, think about it, and maybe ask me a few questions by email the next day. But if they want to, they can sign right there.

And of course, you're paying for lunch.

CHAPTER 7 RECAP: ATTRACTING MILLENNIALS TO JOIN YOUR TEAM

- Write ads that attract millennials to your company culture and to the innate strengths the job requires.
- When you go through the application process yourself and document your responses, you can better hire people who think

and act like you do— people who will make decisions like you would.

- Use a phone interview to weed out candidates that are misaligned, and learn the work history of more promising applicants.
- Simple, specific questions to references insure you get the feedback you need to evaluate the applicant.
- For people with little or no job experience look at sports, volunteer work, or intern work. Rock stars will help you find creative sources to give you feedback.
- Create an interview process that also acts like a "test" for the job. Use their success or failure in the interview as a coaching moment.
- Invite the applicant to a trial day where your team evaluates how well the candidate fits into the company culture.
- When you present the offer, make sure you set expectations and clearly outline in detail what success looks like—what is necessary to achieve milestones, bonuses, commissions, etc.

For a sample of what one of our offer sheets looks like, please visit my website: www.MeetJavierMontes.com

CHAPTER 8

INTEGRATING THE MILLENNIAL INTO YOUR CULTURE

S O FAR WE went through my unique way of attracting, recruiting, and narrowing down choices to pick the right millennial hire. Now that you have hired the new millennial, here are ways to introduce him or her to your culture and totally WOW them, starting on the very first day.

PREPARING FOR THEIR FIRST DAY

How are you going to prepare for their first day so that when they show up, they get a great first experience? In my company, I adapted information from Jack Daly's book, Hyper Sales Growth, and Cameron Herold's method of R & D (Rip Off & Duplicate). Daly's book includes a great deal about welcoming your new hire. We took his process and made it our own. It's very simple and welcoming. We do our best to set their first day on a Friday. Friday is a very loose and relaxed day. It sets the tone for the weekend so it's also an exciting day.

Typically, we take a week before the first day to prepare a few things before the first day of the new hire. One of the most important and impactful things—and one that takes the longest and normally sets us back a little bit—is to have the new hires' business cards ready for their first days. That's a process that has to go to a graphic designer, who has to send the files to their printer; the printer has a certain number of days they need to get the cards ready. This is why their first day should be no less than a week out. You want your new hires' business cards ready and on their new desk when they arrive their first day.

Another thing that we do is to throw a welcoming party. On everybody's first day, we decorate the new hire's workspace. Our company has desks in our common work area and we'll put balloons on his desk… sometimes even a funny tablecloth. We bring the glitter and hang streamers from the ceiling. We decorate the chair as well. This is all part of welcoming them. When they walk through the door on their first day, our entire company stands up and cheers. We play music and clap as they come in as our way to welcome them their first day. On their desk, we normally leave a company polo shirt made especially for them. On their desk, set up nice and ready, we have their business cards, a few company pens, and their laptop.

Every single time that we've hired somebody this way the person has taken a picture and posted it on social media. People send it to all their friends and family because they've never been welcomed to anything like this before. This is an exciting time for them. They've just got a new job that they're very excited about. Then we amp it up to another level so that they really understand how excited we are to bring them on board. This is invaluable to them. Most people have never received an experience like this; they have never been welcomed to any company in this manner. We're setting the tone for the culture they will be experiencing and they understand how important they are going to be to the team.

Another thing that we normally do is bring them some kind of sweets— either a small cake, cupcakes, or something similar—that's waiting for them at their desk when they arrive. The last thing that we do is buy a card, write a nice welcoming note on it, and have all the members of our company sign it. Our company's not that big, so there's enough space for everybody to sign. If your company is bigger, have the members of the department sign it.

Sometimes people open it right then and others take it home to read. The point is that they take something home with them to read and show their friends and family when they tell them how they were welcomed here at the office.

In most businesses, new hires come in without any introduction; they get shown to their cubicle, and their business cards are seldom ready. The way we welcome our new members has a huge impact and gives them a very welcome feeling. They're excited to be part of this team, and they see the culture in action and feel how important they are to the team.

"In a small business, the new hire has a big impact on the organization. If you have ten people, that person is 10 percent of your team; 10% of your entire company. They need to feel valued and important."

In a small business where you have very few employees, the new hire is not just one in the hundreds. They have a big impact on the organization. If you have ten people, for example, that person is 10 percent of your team; 10 percent of your entire company. They need to feel valued and important.

We also take a photo of their welcome and put it on social media so clients and other potential candidates know what a great culture we have and so they can join in welcoming the new hire. There is another big reason why we try to make their first day a Friday. Most of our team spends most of the day welcoming the new person and we normally go out to lunch as a team. It's a fun day. They typically don't get much work done on their first day. Maybe they set up their email, begin to learn about our systems, and create their bio for our website. We usually go home early on Fridays and they get to go back to their world— to their family and their friends. Because this was such a memorable first day, they're going to tell their friends and family how amazing their first day was. They promote the company. They go home knowing that they have made the right decision to join our team.

We have planted the seed of culture in every new employee. Also, it's important to point out that all this work is done before they ever become an employee. This isn't a case of candidates walking in and filling out a job application, and we say, "Great, you've got a pulse. You start tomorrow." I'm trying to enforce culture from the very beginning. I've designed this process so that new hires are engulfed by our culture before they ever enter the building.

Our candidates understand the company's culture isn't something we concocted in a day. It's deep and wide. Years went into defining it. That's why it's important for us to get the right cultural fit between our organization and a new team member. The right people are going to be excited about our vibrant culture. The wrong people will be turned off by it, walk the other way, disappear off the candidate list, and never respond to another email. That's exactly what we want. We know the right cultural fit brings people who amplify and deepen our culture.

The wrong people will kill our culture. I think that's where a lot of small businesses, departments, and entrepreneurs get it wrong. They are trained to hire on skill-set and not on mind-set. They don't ingrain the culture in people's minds before hiring them. They may promote and talk about culture on their website but they really don't bring it to life.

In our company people are exposed to what our culture is from the moment they connect with us. They see it, feel it, breath it, and can clearly make a decision on whether there is a match. Of course this entire process is an investment. We spend a lot of hours and a lot of money getting the right person. However, this investment pays huge dividends. The new hire comes with an attitude and the willingness to learn and work that's tenfold what it would have been had we taken the first attractive resume. We save a tremendous amount in time and training because our turn-over is low to non-existent.

PROMOTING YOUR CULTURE AND YOUR TEAM

Our team is our family, and our culture is the environment. As business owners, leaders, and CEOs, it's our job to promote this culture. We expose all our team to the culture through the hiring process. Then through every other channel possible, we want to let the world know about our culture and put out small feeders to attract the right people to our culture— clients, joint venture partners, strategic partners, or potential employees.

After everything you've done on day one to forge the culture around a new employee who is starting at your company, you need to know how to keep this running. Three months, six months, or two years in, how do you make sure that the shininess doesn't wear off, and now the person dreads Monday and going back to work? This is where we work on promoting the culture and the team.

Through the years, we have tried a few practices within our company to promote our culture. Some have worked much better than other. Here are the top four things that have worked well for us. I encourage all businesses to do them.

Employee Bios

First, all of your employees should have a bio page on your website. This is your family, your team. Every person on your team should have his own little spotlight on your website. Then your customers, potential vendors, or anybody who is interacting with your company can see who is a part of your family and get to know them a bit before meeting them in person. The clients may exchange an email with a team member and wonders what the person looks like, or want to learn more about them. Vendors we do regular business with seldom get to meet the person on the other side of the phone or email. It's always nice to put a face to a name or voice.

While many businesses do some very simple version of this, I have found that they underestimate its importance and seldom invest much time or money in it. Most businesses grossly underestimate the impact a great bio on the website will have on each of your team members. This is such an important tool because most employees have never had a bio page made for them at any of their previous companies. This might be the first time that they have the opportunity to shine and be in the spotlight. Many of them have never had somebody else telling the entire world how great they are and what makes them stand out. Your team will take a lot of pride in this and will promote the bios to everybody they know. They'll say, "Hey, check this out. Look at me on my company page." They are going to spread the word to everyone they know. This person is such an important part of your team, its only right that they get an amazing spotlight on your website.

Wouldn't it make sense to invest in a professional photographer to take really good headshots of that person? If you go to our company's website, you'll see that we take it a bit further and actually make high-quality videos of every person on our team. That way people can see each team member's personality, see them in action, and get a good sense of who they are— instead of just a picture and some words about this person's role on our team. Every company can decide how far it wants to go. This is something that we do at EMG, and it has yielded us amazing results.

Yes, it takes time. Yes, it takes money. Yes, it's a huge investment to undertake this task. But consider the savings in retention rates. In our case, none of our employees ever left voluntarily. That's a huge. We want to keep it that way and all the things that we do for our team pour into that. We want to make our team members understand that we've chosen to work with them, we're very proud to have them on our team, and we want to tell the whole world how amazing they are.

There are other hidden benefits. As your team members share their bio with their friends, email it to family, and put it on all their social media, this is free promotion for your company. It also makes your people feel like celebrities. We ask each of our people to write their own bios so that they can put their own style and personality behind it. We also have them answer a few fun and interesting questions about themselves.

The bio lets us give new hires meaningful work on the first day. We don't want them shadowing all day, because other people might have work to do and can be distracted. Part of our first-day process is to have them take an hour to sit down, read everybody's bios, and then write their own.

They learn more about the team and what they like. This gives them information to use to reach out and say hi to the rest of the team. That helps them integrate faster. There is a lot of value in doing this and making it part of the first-day experience.

Social Media

Second, our culture uses our social media a bit differently than most companies. A lot of companies don't get a lot of business from social media. Our clients don't go on social media and decide they want to work with us simply because they saw some of our work there. That's a very small percentage of people.

But we've learned that people follow us on social media because they really like to see what we're doing and they enjoy seeing our team. Especially if you don't get a lot of business from social media, I recommend that your social media is focused on your team, fun happenings at your company, employee recognitions, and things that highlight your culture and every member of your team. Don't use your social media to continually promote your business. That becomes annoying, and you'll get unfollowed pretty quickly.

Social media became popular because humans are natural voyeurs; they like to get the inside scoop. It's like being able to pull back the curtain and see what's really going on inside a company. That's part of what makes social media really popular and a lot of our followers (who tend to be millennials) like to see what we're doing behind the scenes.

Everybody puts on their website all the wonderful things about them. They put up very professional pictures and perfectly crafted copy of what they think that their clients want to see and read. The truth is that every company has its real culture behind the scenes. This is exciting for people who are active on social media— currently most of the world's population. They like to see this behind-the-scenes life; it's what gets them excited and intrigued about organizations they choose to follow.

We use that as an outlet to promote our culture and our team. If we get a new team member, you'd better believe he is going to be on social media during his first couple of days. If we're doing something cool, something funny, something with the economy, or something that's trending in top news, our company will put it on social media. If somebody deserves to be recognized, we recognize them inside the company. But why not recognize them all over social media? It doesn't matter that it's an internal thing. It doesn't matter if it's a top salesperson for this month or this quarter; the world can know about it, and people will be excited the company is telling the whole world about the accomplishment. Promote the culture and fuel the fire under your entire team, because everybody is going to want to be recognized in the same way.

> **"Our social media followers love it because they engage with what's going on behind the scenes, and our team loves it because they get to be promoted and be put out there for the entire world to see how awesome they truly are. It's a win-win situation for everybody."**

This is how we promote through social media. Our followers love it because they engage with what's going on behind the scenes, and our team loves it because they get to be promoted and be put out there for the entire world to see how awesome they truly are. It becomes a win-win situation for everybody involved.

Not many companies have a culture and a team that they are proud of. Even the ones that do, don't invest their time into broadcasting it. Imagine what it would do for your business if somebody researches your company. When they google you, they stumble across this lively social media presence where people are smart and fun, and the information is current. That will make a huge impression on them when they get to their final buying decision. I can tell you this from first-hand experience. I have received countless comments from our clients about our social media posts even before they chose to do business with us.

When any of our vendors stop by our office, we promote them on social media so it causes the other vendors to want to stop by as well. It's an energy that's continuous and it's such a powerful force.

Most people post their greatest project on social media because they're proud of it and they want to show off the amazing work they do. That's fine, but I wouldn't say that should be the biggest part of your social media presence. Again, social media is meant to be just that: social. It's peeking into the private lives of people or businesses, and seeing what they're doing. They're following you because they want to see what's behind the scenes. They want to know the latest and greatest happenings within your culture, your life, and your company. It's sad that not many organizations are leveraging these platforms and taking advantage of something that is so simple and free!

Family Events

This third idea is also my favorite. Consider the tradition of hosting a few events each year where your team members invite family, significant others, or friends to attend.

When a new member joins our team, they go home and tell families and friends how great our company is, how wonderful the culture is, and how excited they are to be working with us. But these people just have secondhand knowledge— words or social media. Why not give people outside of your organization an opportunity to experience this amazing culture firsthand? Have them come to events where they can see what the company culture is like. This can be very simple and it doesn't need to cost a lot of money. Some simple ideas include hosting a picnic at a park or a little barbecue in your own backyard.

These are very small, easy things that will enforce your culture and let team members' friends, families, and significant others know that this is what your company is all about. This is what your culture is. Yes, we do business, but at the same time, this is how we do business. This is what our environment feels like. This why they wake up every day excited to go to work at our company.

It all comes back to millennials having their personal and work lives intertwined. You help them feel this unity of work and life by hosting a few events— once a quarter, or maybe just twice a year. You bring family into a work setting as your team invites their family or friends to come and participate in your team-building activities.

Trust me, the friends and family will talk about it to all of their friends. They'll go back to their own jobs and tell their coworkers how amazing your culture is and how much fun they had at your events. You create this perpetual loop to promote your own culture and team. At the same time, you develop lifelong team members and create support for your company among their families.

> **"Family activities create this perpetual loop to promote your own culture and team. At the same time, you develop lifelong team members and create support for your company among their families."**

I constantly get the question of what do to during these events. We've done plenty of different things. If we go to a park and do a barbecue, we'll organize a kickball game or something similar, where everybody can participate. On bowling nights where everybody comes along, we do small competitions— keeping it on a friendly level. Prior to the event, we check the demographics of our team's guests and make sure that there's something for everybody to do, so everybody can participate. It makes people feel appreciated and surprised. Typically family events do not always create fun that specifically takes the guests into consideration.

I'm not the most creative person, so if I can plan a fun family event, so can you. The hardest part may be finding a day everyone can attend. So I typically schedule these as far in advance as possible—even a year out. Then we just need to get creative on what can be done and what your team enjoys doing. Keep in mind the interests and abilities of families and guests.

Start by telling your team you want to plan a family fun day. Ask them what they want to do and what they think their families will enjoy. Emphasize that your team is hosting their families, their significant others, and their friends.

Let them buy into it and give their ideas. You don't need to do all the hard work yourself or all the creative thinking. They will tell you what they like. They'll come up with great ideas, and the more they participate, the better it's going to be because they are part of the creation. If they're part of the planning, that means they're all going to go to the event.

Infuse some recognition into the event for even greater impact. You can create an award or a kind of surprise at the event. If there is something someone has achieved, why not take that opportunity to recognize them? There is nothing more powerful than being recognized in front of your entire family. It's huge. There is a balance between recognizing one person versus not recognizing the others, but outstanding performers should always be recognized. It offers motivation. Again, your company culture should be set this way because that's how the world really is.

Millennials are used to everybody getting a trophy, but in business there are winners and losers. With millennials, you can celebrate many small victories, but still recognize the outstanding performers. They need to know outstanding performance will always be rewarded.

The Sun Sentinel hosted an annual awards night that was just like the Grammys or the Oscars. It was a black tie event and they rented out an amazing arena. They had a host and spent the night recognizing people with a big party afterward. People would look forward to the event and those who got awards would put them on their desks. It was a huge part of their culture, and they did it for years. When they were purchased by a new company, they stopped organizing this event, and the team was devastated. Whether it's small or large, these events impact morale and company culture. It's entirely up to you.

The Sun Sentinel had a thousand employees and the event called for a sizeable budget. But that one night— along with all the planning and anticipation— got the team excited and put wind in their sails for an entire year. You'd better believe that if you didn't win anything that night, you came back to work the next day thinking about how you were going to find a way to stand out next year and guarantee an award in front of all your peers and relatives.

SOCIAL RESPONSIBILITY

The last point about attracting and keeping millennials on your team is being socially responsible. If you're not already doing it, start a program to make your company a little more socially or environmentally responsible. This is very important for millennials.

This could be a number of things, and I'm going to give a few examples, but as always, it can be something very small and easy, or very big and time-consuming. The more you get into it, and the more your millennials want it, the more you can build on this.

Recycling

You can create an office recycling program. Millennials value the environment and want to make the world a better place for the generations to come. Start simple. Get a container and label it: Recycling. That's your office's recycling program. If your company is bigger you may need multiple containers. It's an easy way for you to build culture that your company acts responsibly, and cares about the environment and the future.

Previous generations have taken our world for granted and may not take issues such as pollution or global warming seriously. Millennials view this as a very serious topic and they want to be part of companies that share their concerns. Millennials will take part in an office recycling program. Some of them may spearhead it, if you give them the opportunity to lead, because they connect with these kinds of activities and programs.

"Organize volunteer activities, like feeding the homeless, during work hours in order to show that you're really committed to being socially responsible."

Volunteer Activities

You can also promote or organize volunteer activities during work hours. It can be an activity like going to feed the homeless, but it needs to be done during work hours. If you're doing it outside of work hours as a company, that's okay, but in order to show that you're really committed, you should do it during work hours. Your message: "We're going to take some hours during the work time to go out and do this volunteer work as a company. We're giving up our time to be productive on our personal and company goals because we care about other people, because we care about feeding the homeless, because we care about providing clothing for the people who don't have anything to wear."

There are all kinds of things that you can do and many organizations with which you can partner. Other ideas include cleaning beaches or highways. The key point is for this to be done during work hours to show your commitment and be generally accepted among your team.

Donate to Charities. This idea is relatively easy. Find out what charities are important to the millennials on your team and donate money from the company to them. Sometimes the prize for a company contest could be for the company to make a donation to the charity of the winner's choice. Or perhaps the winner of a team event gets a bonus and at the same time you donate an equal amount to the charity of the winner's choice.

Things of this nature motivate and stimulate the millennials on your team. Of course, you want to promote all of this on your social media. This is a part of promoting your culture and your team. They will tell the whole world about socially responsible events and will feel very proud to be part of your company. This attracts other millennials to come work for you.

You can see examples of this happening today by simply turning on the TV or reading top news in any search engine page. This is all over the media on any given day. The moment a big oil company has an oil spill, for example, it blows up everywhere. Millennials grab this and boycott the company. They get very passionate about these situations and start a revolution against a company who is not being socially responsible or is harming the environment.

If we know how important this is to millennials, we should adjust our companies and create things that will attract and excite them.

Millennials will actually consider leaving a company that is not socially responsible to go work for you, if they see that you're actively trying to preserve the environment and help those who are less fortunate.

Again, you have to back this up with action. You can't just talk the talk—you need to walk the walk. A fellow entrepreneur, James Ashcroft wrote the book The Best Me: From Couch Potato to Long Distance Triathlete, And The Discovery Of What Matters Most In Life. In his book, Ashcroft talks about how he uses a 4-step process to discover what matters most in life. Today, he uses this system to raise money for various causes that he is passionate about while running marathons and Iron Man races. Again, just another example of how we can get creative with activities that we can incorporate in our organizations. Incorporate some of these very simple activities (or larger, like James's marathons) or programs into your culture, and you'll get a huge return on your investment from your millennials. They're going to support your organization and its efforts and promote your company even more because they'll share your beliefs. Again, they're going to be dedicated to a company that is contributing and truly giving back to the world.

In our company, we don't actively promote this to new potential hires. They will see everything we do when they come in the door. We see it as a way to show them a little more icing on the cake after they have been hired, so they'll fall in love with the company even more.

Sometimes your own team has already promoted the team's socially responsible activities and attracted somebody to join your team because of that. The word about anything you're doing spreads very quickly. It might be that for somebody, your environmentally and socially responsible activities are the main reasons that they have decided to explore an opportunity with your company.

Chapter 8 Recap: Integrating the Millennial into Your Culture

- Make their first day such a fantastic welcome they're convinced they've made the right decision and they tell everyone how great your company is.
- Promote your company culture through social media.
- Use family events to bring work and personal life together and make work more fun.
- Create a socially responsible environment by doing things like recycling, volunteering during company time, or donating to charity to attract and keep millennials.

For the most up-to-date material and additional information on millennials and to watch quick videos that dive deeper into these concepts, please visit my website: www.MeetJavierMontes.com

CHAPTER 9

THE LEADERSHIP ROLE MODEL

IN A SMALL business or a huge company, the CEO is the key person of
the organization. Leaders need to present themselves in a different way
now that millennials are becoming the largest segment of the workforce.

BE THE POSTER CHILD

This chapter helps you understanding what your role is in the company
and how millennials view us. How do we fulfill that role for millennials?
I think they view CEO as being the ultimate poster child for the
company and the company's culture.

The book *Traction*, by Gino Wickman, reinforces the idea that the
visionary of the company should be in charge of its culture. It says
the company leader should develop the company's culture, enforce it,
and make sure that it stays alive throughout the entire organization.
Millennials look for this. It needs to be vibrant and alive for them to
click with it. As you fulfill this role, millennials will look up to you and
want to follow and stand behind you.

The CEO is the person they are looking to and who they want to lead
them. In a large company it could be the organization leader. Millennials
want to learn from this person. They need access to the top so that they
can get firsthand information and see and feel the inspiration that flows
directly from this leader. Millennials crave a personal connection to the
top. They want this person to have big dreams and move the company

or the department forward to achieve them. Millennials dream very big and have no limits. Their dreams are exponential because they grew up in a time when they were seeing their peers become multi-billionaires. For them, there is nothing that's out of reach. They want to be led by somebody who has the exact same type of vision, drive, and motivation. A millennial needs to be able to fulfill his or her life's purpose at work as well as at home.

"You need somebody who is inspirational, who is motivational, who has big dreams, and who can lead millennials down that path to fulfill them as people and as a part of your company."

What if your company is very large? This is easily scalable. Don't try to force it. The leader must be sincere and genuine because people can read through someone who is trying to fake it. Maybe as the CEO or the president of the company, you don't feel you're that person. That's okay. But you need to have somebody in the forefront who can be that person. You need somebody who is inspirational, who is motivational, who has big dreams, and who can lead millennials down that path to fulfill them as people and as a part of your company. It's important to understand what the role is in order to see whether or not we are that person. Smaller companies usually have this visionary leader. When we start businesses, the dream is in our heads, and typically defines us as one of our passions. For larger organizations, we may or may not be that person. Look for somebody in the company who can be that cheerleader, that poster child, that motivation and inspiration for the millennials to look up to and follow. Again, millennials want to be led; they don't want to be managed.

Millennials look to their leaders in a different way than previous generations. Other generations probably wanted somebody who inspired and motivated them, but big corporate America believed the CEO was untouchable and unreachable. You must wade through a number of other leaders or management levels before you can interact with this person. However, leaders like Richard Branson have successfully gotten to the frontline, hung out, and spent the day with their entire team, regardless of where workers fell in the hierarchy of his organization.

Millennials are demotivated by a CEO who locks himself in his penthouse office and doesn't interact with his frontline workers or the middle managers. Millennials need access to the top so they can voice their opinions and ask their questions. As leaders, we should facilitate that. Some companies have held all-company meetings, where anybody can ask questions and give comments or opinions. Those are steps in the right direction to embrace the millennial generation. If you are a huge organization, this may be the way to do it. I don't expect everybody to have access to the leader of a company every single day, but there should be a channel or a process to reach that person so that millennials can interact.

Because millennials want to have the inside scoop, open-book management and town hall meeting have become very popular. They feel fulfilled when they can actually hear leaders, know what's going on within the organization, and get the latest and greatest news. If they are not involved in this, they feel marginalized and like they are left out of the loop. Every company is different, and every company will decide to embrace or engage this as much as they want.

Books like *The Great Game of Business* by Jack Stack and Bo Burlingham have talked about these concepts for years. This generation is simply requiring these concepts be implemented. Millennials are putting our feet to the fire and saying, "This is what we want or we go someplace else."

It's no longer a competitive advantage, but a requirement.

MILLENNIALS WANT TO LEARN FROM YOU

I've mentioned many times how important learning is for millennials. They're not looking for money. They're not looking to get their nine to five done and then go home and forget about work. They're not purposely trying to disconnect from work when they're not at the office. What they want is to learn. They want access to your knowledge and everything you can teach them.

"If you take the time to teach them, if you take the time to coach them, and if you take the time to develop them, millennials will be much more loyal to you than you could ever imagine."

If you take the time to teach them, if you take the time to coach them, and if you take the time to develop them, they will be much more loyal to you than you could ever imagine. You overcome any fear you might have of them leaving after you increase their value by sharing with them everything you know. You will gain a long-term supporter and a fierce and motivated team member.

Also, by teaching, coaching, and developing them, you'll be investing in building a highly qualified team that will be able to take on any challenge. It will also take a load off your shoulders because you'll have people around you who know how to handle situations and make decisions the way you would. You will no longer be solely responsible for solving all the problems.

If you ask me, everyone wins when you take the time to coach and teach your millennials— and the rest of your team as well.

MILLENNIALS WANT TO BE INSPIRED BY YOU

Let's be honest. Even the most exciting job can get dull if the energy in the workplace is low. Conversely, even tasks that might seem tedious can be turned into as much fun as a trip to Disney World® with the right attitude and leadership. Millennials want Disney World® every day, and they expect you to take them there. They want to look up to you as their main source of inspiration, as the person who can get them pumped up about every aspect of their day—their goals, the projects they're leading, the social responsibility programs at your company, and everything in between.

Take some of your time to be the person who provides their daily dose of inspiration. Your millennials will trust you know how to accomplish things. They'll believe you're excited about the company, its growth, its team, and most importantly, its culture. They'll stay excited when they know each day they come into the office, they will get to spend time being inspired by you. Excited millennials are more productive, more imaginative, more pumped up, and more creative about how to get things done and exceed the expectations you set for them.

DREAM BIG WITH THEM

Dreams are a big part of a millennial's life. They were encouraged to dream ever since they were children, and they keep on doing it on a daily basis. They dream about everything: the house they want to live in, the dog they'll adopt, the places they want to see. And of course, they dream about the professional and personal goals they want to achieve.

If they see that your dreams are not as big as theirs, it can be very demotivating for them. They'll start doubting their purpose, especially if they get the feeling that you're not dreaming big and are perfectly happy where you are. They dream about advancing, developing, and continuously improving. When looking up to you, they expect nothing less. They want your dreams to be as big as (or even bigger than) theirs. They want to be challenged and inspired by what you dream of achieving.

Don't forget that there's nothing too big, too complicated, or impossible to achieve in the minds of millennials. For years, we loved the idea of having an advisory board, but always believed that we were too small. This pre-conceived notion was shattered after reading Marissa Levin's book, Built to Scale: How Top Companies Create Breakthrough Growth Through Exceptional Advisory Boards. Once we implemented this, our entire team was motivated and felt challenged to see what other big dream we could tackle next!

Be Sincere About Your Purpose

Not having a purpose is not an acceptable situation for millennials. I dedicated quite a bit of space in this book to explaining why it's so important that they know exactly what their roles and purpose are in the company. Now we need to address the fact that they also want to know about your purpose.

This connects a few different concepts about millennials— the desire for good communication and having access to the inside scoop. It also connects to inspiration, motivation, and structure. Knowing your purpose gives you credibility in your millennials' eyes; because it helps them better understand these things about you and your relationship to them.

- How you can help them
- What you can teach them
- What role you play in the company
- What requests they can expect to receive from you

It's vital you are sincere about your purpose. You may need to dig deep to uncover it and you must understand your purpose and vision. Don't try to make a special version of it for your millennials' sake. They are intuitive and observant and will know if you are not being entirely honest with them. They'd much rather know the not-so-comfortable truth than the beautiful but false projection.

CARE ABOUT THEM PERSONALLY

When millennials think about their lives, the personal and professional aspects of it are in no way separated. They come to consider the office as a second home, and they see their team members (which include you) as a family. They don't expect to be best friends with everybody, but they do wish you, as their supervisor and leader, care about them as a person and not only as an employee.

"If you create vision, excitement and care about them as people, the final result will amaze you. A fulfilled millennial will demonstrate passion, willingness to work, to learn, and to improve that is not easily equaled."

They crave personal connections at the workplace, and that includes you too. They want you to show interest in the big things that are going on in their lives: whether they seem sad or happy, or whether they are sick or going on vacation. In the same way, they'll come to care about you. They are looking for a mutual relationship. And they definitely don't want to feel like a number in a spreadsheet or the number of sales they make per month.

If you care about them as people, along with the other recommendations in this chapter, the final result will amaze you. A fulfilled millennial's passion and willingness to work, to learn, and to improve is not easily equaled. They will change your day-to-day in ways you would never expect.

CHAPTER 9 RECAP: THE LEADERSHIP ROLE MODEL

- The leader sets the company culture and enforces it throughout the entire organization.
- Millennials need a leader they can have access to, look up to, and follow.

- When you take the time to teach, coach, and develop millennials they will be extremely loyal to you.
- Millennials want vision and inspiration from their leaders.
- Millennials want to know your purpose, your dreams, and your desires for growth.
- The best leaders care about their team as individuals in addition to their worth on the team.

For additional details on the characteristics of millennials and to watch quick videos that dive deeper into each of these, please visit my website: www.MeetJavierMontes.com

MILLENNIALS AND THE REST OF YOUR TEAM

CURRENTLY, THE WORKFORCE is made up of different generations: millennials (Generation Y), Generation X, and baby boomers. It's been popularized that boomers, Gen Xers, and millennials can have discord when it comes to management, views on life, and definitions of success. How will incorporating the ideas outlined in this book be received by all generations throughout the company?

How Will the Rest of Your Team Feel About All This?

This is a question I get asked a lot. All the concepts I've been talking about throughout this book sound great for millennials, but how is this going to affect the rest of the team? How will the rest of the team feel about all this, if we are catering just to the millennials? My answer is pretty simple. If we go back and look at everything that we've talked about in this book— everything millennials want, everything that motivates and challenges them—it's very much in line with what every other generation has wanted as well. Other generations have always wanted their work to have meaning, value, and purpose. Every generation has wanted their strengths to be utilized in the company and has wanted to be acknowledged and praised. Every generation has wanted to feel like they are a part of a team that's bigger than them and can accomplish big goals. Every generation has wanted to follow a leader, and nobody has ever wanted to be micromanaged. Every generation would love to have fun at work, but maybe they've not been able to, or haven't been given the permission to.

Every generation has some small bit of entrepreneurial spirit in them. All people, at some point in their lives, have thought about possibly having their own company or having a small side business that they would like to operate on their own. None of these things are exclusive to millennials. Who doesn't want to get more praise from their supervisor at work? Who wouldn't like to collaborate more with their coworkers, if they get along well and are now friends? If you develop the right culture with the right team, and that's all aligned with your core values, it will make sense that more people are going to get along and develop stronger friendships because they have more things in common. They think the same and act the same.

"If you develop the right culture with the right team, then people from all generations will get along and develop stronger friendships because they have more things in common."

What's been happening, in my experience, is that millennials are grabbing onto these concepts and making them required standards, instead of thinking they are optional in life and at work. Millennials seek environments that embrace these concepts before fully committing themselves. Business leaders need to look at their organizations and make sure that they create this type of environment, not just for millennials, but for people of all generations; it's what they want, too. Perhaps previous generations were conditioned to accept the status quo. Maybe previous generations said, "I have settled for this job because I was raised thinking that I need to stay with that company for thirty years, whether I like it or not. I was raised in a time when I had to go to work, even though I don't necessarily like my job; I just go, work, clock out, come home, and then live my life."

The millennial generation is blatantly bringing all these things to the forefront. They are not shy about saying that their priority is not to work, but to have happy lives and to go after the things that they want. They want companies and organizations that provide them these things. Until they find these organizations, they'll keep searching; they don't feel the need to stay with organizations that don't foster the environment that's conducive to their happiness. This disruptive change of the last few years is something everybody in your organization is going to love. Your whole team will feel energized.

The big takeaway is that these strategies are not just for millennials—they work for everybody.

REIGNITE THE START-UP MIND-SET OR CULTURE

An added bonus that millennials bring to any organization they join is that they instinctively help to reignite the start-up mind-set and culture. If you let them, they will bring that fire back into your organization—even if it's been stagnant for years. If you are setting your year goals to grow 10 percent, why not grow 50 percent? It doesn't matter if that's something you have never done before. Bring in innovative thinking. Bring in millennials who will challenge you to dream big. Reigniting that fire throughout your entire organization, regardless of its size, will yield huge benefits! It's time to bring that start-up mind-set back into the company. Technology and methods change so rapidly today we need millennials to come in and teach us other ways—new, different, better, unusual ways. I urge you to challenge all the things you are currently doing. Be open to change. Most large organizations today, that have been around for a long time, find it difficult to make any change, to move such a big lever. It's so much work that many companies won't even try. These companies may end up non-competitive or dead.

Re-igniting the start-up mind-set aligns everyone in your company with the idea of dreaming big. It opens their minds to the possibility of exponential growth. If you can reignite that fire across your entire team, there is a big chance that you can accomplish those goals. Once you do, everybody will feel so much more empowered and united. They will want to do even bigger things the next year. You will attract more top talent into your team because you are doing such amazing things in your industry. You will be surrounded by people who are positive, optimistic, and action oriented, and who say, "Let's go do it!" They'll have a leadership team behind them that says, "We are behind you. We are going to support you. We are going to mentor and coach you. Let's go do it together. We are a team, and we are going to build this organization together while having a great time." Everybody wants to be a part of that.

Challenge Your Current Systems and Processes

Most companies, big or small, follow the same processes and implement the same systems baby boomers established. I hope this book proves to you the time has come to take advantage of the innovation and ideas that millennials are bringing to the workplace and that you allow yourself to review every system and process in your organization.

This doesn't mean that the systems and processes you have in place aren't good. They are and were part of your success for many years. But the world is changing and we should change with it. Leveraging technology to update your current systems and processes will make you more competitive, dynamic, and more profitable.

"Leveraging technology suggested by millennials to update your current systems and processes will make you more competitive, dynamic, and more profitable."

The concepts in this book will inspire your team members—all generations of them. These concepts will also help you walk the path of an amazing example your entire team will be excited to follow. Once they see your intention to advance and improve, they'll start thinking how they can advance and improve in their roles as well. They'll begin to come up with ideas that will help improve your company, openly share feedback, and feel excited to be a part of a company that's truly changing and making a difference in the world. These concepts, brought to light by the millennial generation, have completely transformed my organization for the better, united my entire team, helped us leverage the use of technology, and most importantly, helped us experience exponential growth in all aspects of our business. My only hope is that this book will help to do the same for you.

Chapter 10 Recap: Millennials and the Rest of Your Team

- Every generation wants their work to have meaning and purpose. They want their strengths to be recognized and use by the company. They want to be part of a team that accomplishes grand goals. They want work to be fun.
- The strategies in this book are not just for millennials, they work for everyone.
- Millennials will ignite the start-up mind-set of big goals and big dreams that can change and grow your business.
- Use millennials to help you innovate processes and systems to make you more competitive, dynamic, and profitable.

For the most up-to-date material and additional information on millennials and to watch quick videos that dive deeper into these concepts, please visit my website: www.MeetJavierMontes.com

Made in the USA
San Bernardino, CA
13 July 2017